From the Principal's X-Files

The Unexpected Tales of a Practical Principal

Deana Hollaway and Werner M. Hollaway

ROWMAN & LITTLEFIELD EDUCATION
Lanham • New York • Toronto • Plymouth, UK

Published in the United States of America
by Rowman & Littlefield Education
A Division of Rowman & Littlefield Publishers, Inc.
A wholly owned subsidiary of The Rowman & Littlefield Publishing Group, Inc.
4501 Forbes Boulevard, Suite 200, Lanham, Maryland 20706
www.rowmaneducation.com

Estover Road
Plymouth PL6 7PY
United Kingdom

British Library Cataloguing in Publication Information Available

Library of Congress Cataloging-in-Publication Data

Hollaway, Deana, 1962–
   From the principal's X-files : the unexpected tales of a practical principal / Deana
Hollaway and Werner M. Hollaway.
      p. cm.
   Includes bibliographical references.
   ISBN-13: 978-1-57886-954-1 (cloth : alk. paper)
   ISBN-10: 1-57886-954-4 (cloth : alk. paper)
   ISBN-13: 978-1-57886-955-8 (pbk. : alk. paper)
   ISBN-10: 1-57886-955-2 (pbk. : alk. paper)
   ISBN-13: 978-1-57886-956-5 (electronic)
   ISBN-10: 1-57886-956-0 (electronic)
   1. Elementary school principals—United States. 2. Educational leadership—United
States. I. Hollaway, Werner M., 1953– II. Title.

   LB2831.92.H65 2009
   371.2'012—dc22   2008036720

∞™ The paper used in this publication meets the minimum requirements of
American National Standard for Information Sciences—Permanence of
Paper for Printed Library Materials, ANSI/NISO Z39.48-1992.
Manufactured in the United States of America.

Contents

Foreword

Back in 1970 I started my education career as a second-grade teacher in Avon Park, Florida. Now many years later and several education-related jobs later, there are things I wish all educators could know. Much of this is the information that you did not learn in the college classes or school district professional development programs, but gleaned through life experiences on the job as a school leader.

Deana and Werner have captured much of this information in *From the Principal's X-Files*. Together, this sister and brother duo has managed to make me have tears of laughter and compassion while reading the vignettes of their years of real-life experiences as school leaders. They offer a compelling view of situations that school leaders might encounter that were not taught in a classroom setting. Their firsthand accounts offer hope and insight for novice and sage educators alike. The child-centered approach to education that Deana and Werner take will serve as a great reminder for school leaders as to the importance of their role on the school campus. I feel confident that readers will feel inspired and motivated by the words that follow.

Grace G. Thomas, EdD
Former: Assistant Superintendent of Putnam Public Schools, Florida
District Relations Specialist, Success for All Foundation,
Baltimore, Maryland
School Improvement Consultant, Southern Regional Education Board,
Atlanta, Georgia
CDDRE Consultant, Johns Hopkins University, Baltimore, Maryland

Acknowledgments

I am grateful to so many people for providing inspiration and acumen for my part of this book. First, thank you to all the wonderful school leaders whom I have had the pleasure to work with including Cecil, Ronnie, Joe, Will, Randy, Garner, Gia, Billy, Jim, Henry, Micky, Vince, Casey, Glen, and Debbie. My gratitude also goes to the other administrators, school counselors, and teachers who were willing to share their perspectives with me. I am honored to work with people who dedicate their lives to teaching children. I am appreciative to everyone on the school campus who strives to make a difference in the lives of children. Their influence can also be seen in the pages that follow.

I am also indebted to my brother, Werner Hollaway, whose infinite knowledge on the subject is evident throughout these pages. As my older brother, I have always looked up to him. As a best friend, confidante, and colleague, he has made a tremendous impact on my life. I also want to express my sincere appreciation to Dr. Grace Thomas for her willingness to write about the chapters within this work. His insight into teaching, parenting, and working with children provides a framework for our own efforts. Special thanks also goes to Dave for agreeing to be a sounding board, a fresh set of eyes and ears, and a support system for me as the book came together. I also want to thank Dana Downs whose friendship and support made this work so much easier for me to pursue over the past year. Lastly, thank you to my son, Jonathan; you continue to be my greatest inspiration.—Deana

Words pale in accurately describing the depth of my gratitude and appreciation for all of those who have nurtured and supported my efforts as an educator, counselor, and school administrator over the years. First and foremost, I would like to thank my wife and soul mate, Catherine, for the countless evenings she selflessly and lovingly spent (after working a full day herself) parenting our children as I furthered my education and later spent long hours at my schools attempting to make a positive difference in the lives of the children of others. Her sacrifice, support, and unfaltering love have made every success in all my endeavors possible.

Secondly, I am thankful and blessed to have experienced the love, patience, and support of my children, Christa, Nicole, Leaa, and Justin as we traveled along this life's path learning and growing together. I am proud of the children they have been and the human beings and adults they have grown to become. In their lives, the best is yet to be. Along the professional path that I have traveled over the years, I would be remiss if I did not acknowledge the opportunities to grow, learn, and develop as a human being and helping professional that I have shared with the thousands of students, hundreds of teachers and staffs of schools, and scores of administrators (both school and district support level) throughout my near thirty years in education. These combined experiences have helped define my life's purpose and mission. For these experiences and our work together, I am profoundly grateful.

Lastly, I would like to acknowledge and extend my love and gratitude to my sister, Dr. Deana Hollaway, whose vision, support, and counsel over the years created the seeds from which this work has grown. First, as siblings sharing common early experiences, and later as counseling colleagues, our lives have been inextricably bound and shaped to help others. It is my sincere hope that this work in some way will help others to establish and nurture the depth and quality of human experiences that will enhance their professional endeavors in making a positive significant difference in the lives of others. I truly believe the promise of brighter futures is ultimately built upon the foundation of an enduring quality of the connections and relationships we create and nurture between ourselves and others in every aspect of our daily lives. Help others realize their dreams through your work and "Carpe Diem!"—Werner

Chapter One

Introduction:
Why New Principals Need Advice

A funny thing happened on the way to school that first morning. As I (Werner) drove the same familiar path to school as I had for the past eight years, day in and day out, I realized just short of pulling into the parking lot, I had made a wrong turn. Lost in thought and engrossed in the excitement of my first day as principal of my new school, the automatic pilot that is routine and habit took me to the wrong place. Just days prior, the superintendent had called me in his office and offered me a new post as a first-year principal of one of the district's most established and prestigious elementary schools.

We had a lengthy discussion regarding the school's faculty and staff, the student population and its future challenges, along with the school's many academic accomplishments and instructional successes over the recent years. The outgoing principal had been a fixture at the school for over fifteen years. Most of the school's successes and the reputation it enjoyed within the community were directly attributable to that principal's stable and consistent leadership after a distinguished career of over thirty-nine years in public education. The following day (a Friday), the superintendent and I went to the school to meet with my new staff for the first time. Following a brief introduction by the superintendent, I was given the opportunity to address the faculty and staff for the first time as its new educational leader. I must admit it was a very heady and exciting day.

That day, the reality and magnitude of this new assignment truly set in for the first time. After a sleepless Sunday night of apprehension, excited anticipation, nervousness, and yes, a little fear, I "dressed for success" and proceeded to drive to my new school, eager to begin my first principalship. Literally thousands of ideas and thoughts raced through my mind during that drive. Would I be equal to the challenges that came my way? Would the staff embrace the changing of the guard that I represented? Could I motivate, challenge, and lead this accomplished instructional staff to the highest levels of performance possible in an effort to help every child realize academic, social, and emotional success?

Lost in my thoughts, I had driven fifteen miles out of my way before I realized I was driving to my old school. Lucky for me, I was so anxious to get to my new school that I had left thirty minutes earlier than I needed to; thus, no one would ever know of my unintended detour. I caught my mistake just prior to pulling into the parking lot of my old school, made the appropriate directional corrections, and proceeded on my way to my new school. Suddenly, as I pulled into its parking lot toward the parking space marked "Principal," an old familiar saying ran through my mind: "Let the games begin!"

Just as a little background, know that I received this new appointment nine weeks into the school year, the superintendent and I had met with the staff that previous Friday, and I began my new assignment on the following Monday. As I walked into the building, I was immediately met by the school secretary who said:

> Good morning. We have called all the substitutes on the list and still have one classroom yet to cover before the school day begins; what would you like me to do? Shall I ask the guidance counselor, media specialists, PE teacher, or music teacher to cancel their scheduled activities for the day and take over Ms. Smith's class? Should we divide her class into groups of three and send them to be shared among the six other classes on that grade level for the day? Would you like me to let our PTO president or a volunteer who is here for the day take the class? Or do you have another suggestion as to how we can handle the situation?

In that very moment, I realized "there's an awful lot they didn't tell me before they handed me the keys to the schoolhouse!" This unexpected decision was just the beginning of the "baptism by fire" that all new principals experience as they settle into their first assignment as a school's chief executive officer, and ultimately, premier educational leader. During your first moments as a principal, you must be decisive and confident; yet, you must avoid the appearance of unfairness or heavy-handedness. You must exhibit sound educational judgment, while being cognizant of the dynamics of human interactions among your staff and the informal leadership that exists within your school.

What appears to be a relatively simple decision, if handled the wrong way, can undermine your leadership efforts and hamper the potential for what you and your staff can accomplish together in both the short and long run. Every decision you make from this point forward has the potential to unify or divide your staff. Your words and actions will, at best, motivate, guide, and support your staff toward the optimal achievement of common goals, or they will fragment the staff, undermine shared goals, and be counterproductive to the common vision you share together. Hopefully, your previous education, experiences, training, and other preparation has provided you with the requisite skills, abilities, and understanding to be equal to the challenges incumbent upon today's educational leaders.

To be successful in the role of a new principal, the practical principal will want to know who the formal and informal leaders are in the school. The well-informed administrator will know how decisions were made at the school under the previous administration and what procedures have been established previously to deal with common or reoccurring issues. He or she will need to know (or will need to learn) the past practice histories of everything from curriculum, to scheduling, to grading, to student discipline, to parent involvement, to school-based budgeting, and to school-based goal-setting. Failure to obtain this knowledge will certainly undermine an otherwise effective principal's leadership efforts in the beginning and throughout a principal's assignment at a school.

Today's principal faces challenges from a multitude of directions. That individual must be up-to-date on all issues confronting educators of the twenty-first-century. The "No Child Left Behind" legislation, the "IDEA Law," and "PL94-142" are just a few of the constraints which exert profound influence over school-based decision making in public education on a daily basis. The twenty-first century principal must be a curriculum leader, must understand and be well-versed in educational best practices across subject areas, and must be an effective manager to help guide the best instructional outcomes at his or her school day in and day out. He or she must have knowledge and understanding of the achievement data of the school over time as well as a detailed understanding of the demographic mix of the student population of the school.

Recently, improved student performance has been the mantra of elected governmental officials, the business sector, our communities, and our students' parents. In today's educational world, schools are graded right along with students. A school's funding has been directly tied to its efficacy in improving student performance over time. Our schools succeed or fail according to the student population's achievement on standardized tests. Failure to improve student performance over time can result in a principal's transfer or demotion. In some cases, this same failure can result in the restaffing of a school, or even its permanent closure. Our schools, principals, and teachers are more accountable now for their efforts than they have ever been in the history of public education.

In conjunction with these real-world challenges facing today's principal, school leaders must find a way to build lasting, effective connections between every stakeholder within the school's community to enhance their combined efforts in realizing their shared goals and optimal desired institutional outcomes. In the words of Roland Barth, Professor Emeritus of Harvard School of Education, "no single indicator of what the school community can accomplish together is more predictive of their future success in accomplishing its goals than the quality of the relationships that exist within it." Simply put, the practical principal must not only understand the nature of the relationships that exist within the school's community, he or she must also enhance all stakeholders' capacities to connect to each other, their common shared goals, and the vision they have established together.

Throughout this book, a guiding principle to the insights that will be shared is a single-minded focus on building a school's capacity to enhance the connections between administrators and teachers, teachers and students, staff and parents, and the school and its community. When all actors feel positively and qualitatively connected to each other and the goals they are attempting to achieve, the school will be able to realize its goals and perform to its utmost potential. The accomplished principal will, through his decision making and leadership, help create the facilitative conditions under which the school community can grow, flourish, and effectively evolve to meet or exceed the ever-changing demands to make public education relevant and responsive to the varied needs of every student.

Today's principal, if properly prepared, will help a school realize its vision and accomplish its mission. That individual will build capacity for success within the school's culture and effectively steer the learning community through any and all change or challenge that confronts it. In short, the sophisticated principal will lead the learning community toward the success it strives to achieve each and every day. These are some of "the things they did not tell you when they gave you the keys to the schoolhouse."

This guide offers tips to help administrators become more practical principals. Even though most new principals have advanced degrees in administration, they can be unexpectedly blindsided by various issues that arise when they are new on the job. The circumstances that novice administrators encounter can be serious, difficult, yet oftentimes hilarious, bordering on the ludicrous. This pragmatic handbook will help school leaders prepare for dealing with the unpredictable circumstances that often take place in the hallowed halls of education.

Despite the on-the-job training that most new school administrators have received as assistant principals or in other positions, the unusual occurrences that can take place may just push a rookie administrator over the edge. Personal, political, and legal ramifications can ensue with serious consequences. In fact, if a situation is not handled properly, such situations can be fatal professionally and detrimental to one's home life. *From the Principal's X-Files* offers insight into the inner workings of a school to lessen the toll that such an awesome role may take.

Beginning with personnel controversies involving faculty, staff, substitutes, maintenance workers, counselors, and the all-important assistant principals, we (Deana and I) seek to help guide administrators through unknown territories. After all, working with people takes finesse, and how better to hone those skills than already having some awareness of how to deal with the unexpected. Wading through office matters can often take school leaders into murky waters. Because dealing effectively with all the members of an organization is critical in running a school, those matters make up the first five chapters of this book.

Having a well-educated and highly qualified faculty is not enough for the school to run efficiently. The faculty frequently needs direction and strong leadership to stay on the right course. Educators seem to be by nature strong-willed and opinionated, which is not necessarily a bad thing since they are responsible for educating young people, but providing guidance for teachers is not always smooth sailing. The direction may be fraught with controversy and challenged with regard to matters of opinion as far as which direction to take.

Navigating the course for staff members also takes care. From cafeteria workers to aides, these employees are stakeholders who may rebel if they feel unappreciated or overworked. The importance of each individual on the campus should not be overlooked. Every adult in the school building has a role that impacts children. To help everyone in fulfilling their duties in a positive manner, the practical principal will tread carefully. Leadership skills and acumen contribute to how efficiently others carry out their function.

The new sensible principal realizes that not everyone will be pleased with the decisions made. The next chapter of the guide will take principals through some difficult issues that they may have to confront with the changing of the guard. It may be surprising, but not all faculty members may be willing to accept the new school leadership. Overcoming the need to please others all the time will prove invaluable. The decision-making process will go much smoother when school leaders focus on doing what is right for the students. From the building logistics to the legal quandaries that educators can get themselves into, the practical principal must be determined to take a student-driven approach to problem solving.

Resolving conflicts is only one of many skills that the practical principal will benefit from. Not all staff members get along all of the time and when the cafeteria workers have a conflict with each other, a virtual crisis can ensue. The second chapter looks at the funny and serious sides of resolving conflicts between staff members. The school leader will be called upon to wield inspirational tactics to ensure that the school functions smoothly on a daily basis. From unhappy paraprofessionals to bickering teachers, the skilled principal does not seek to divide and conquer, but to unite and strengthen.

Strength will not come from a heavy hand; rather an even one that anticipates disasters, unique needs, and the hilarity that life itself can throw one in. This guide will serve as a compass for principals and other educators. The waters (and words) may sometimes be deep, but the goal is the same—to educate and prepare children for the future. Such services cannot and will not be provided effectively without considering the chapters that follow.

There is so much to say about substitutes that an entire chapter is devoted to the topic. Although it should not surprise any educator or parent, it may be somewhat alarming and disturbing. Substitute teachers have been cleared with background checks, but some do not seem to realize or be aware that they are going to be in the classroom with CHILDREN. From what subs wear to what they do and say, this chapter will share horror stories about subs and give advice on how to avoid further scares.

The chapter questioning the counselor's mental health is meant to raise questions about the expectations that educators, parents, students, and counselors themselves have of the school counselor's role. The counselors' plates are full, yet everyone (from staff to parents) seems to expect more and more from them. From counseling students to scheduling and everything in between, the stress can be overwhelming, even for sage counselors. This chapter explores how to get the best from your counselor, without pushing one of the school's best resources over the edge. Reading coaches and media specialists are included in this mix.

The section dealing with assistant principals reviews key points that are crucial to helping the practical principal allow the second in command to take charge. Assistant principals can be invaluable assets when principals train, supervise, and delegate. In addition, the second in command must be given enough latitude to perform the role effectively. If an assistant principal is not allowed to make decisions without constantly consulting the school principal, his opinion may come to mean very little. Teachers learn very quickly who the decision makers are. They may begin to skip past those whose resolve is not steadfast or timely. An indecisive assistant may be viewed as powerless and lacking in self-confidence.

Today's new school leaders must have the vision to delegate responsibilities to gain the most from everyone on the school campus. When the marks come in with regard to testing, principals and schools must be sure that they measure up. High-stakes testing is a fact of life in schools. Delving into the ever-changing measures and requirements, this chapter will explain what some of the assessments mean. Tips for improving test scores will also be discussed. Test results are not necessarily indicators of bad teaching methods, nor are the results indicative of excellence in all academic areas. They merely examine certain areas of achievement and learning, yet today so much seems to be riding on the outcome of testing.

If test scores do not meet certain standards, schools may be placed on watch lists like academic alert, academic caution, or even be taken over by the state officials. Due to the significant weight placed on testing, it is important to discuss its necessity and function, without forgetting the ultimate goal of providing an education for all children. This section will, therefore, discuss the value of testing and some of the shortcomings of the testing frenzy. Administrators will be given advice on how to handle the pressure of high-stakes testing and steering faculty in the right direction. The astute principal must anticipate the pressures when the waters seem too deep, or currents too rough.

Speaking of rough waters, living in today's society of technological advances, educators must prepare young people to be able to traverse the information highway safely. Young people are often already technologically savvy, so staff members must be one step ahead of them. From Internet safety to integrating technology in the classroom, the chapter on technology offers an in-depth look at appropriate and inappropriate uses of technology in the schools.

Educating America's children to become the competitive leaders of tomorrow is a costly endeavor. Everything comes at a price and the rise in the cost of teaching in America's schools can be astounding. From fundraisers to having no funds, the chapter on budgets addresses important financial concerns for the frugal administrator to consider. Many school leaders may begin and end their tenure in an aging facility, and even if they do not, their ultimate goal is to put as much funding into direct services to children, rather than the facility. Such financial decisions, though, can be very difficult to make at times.

With toilets overflowing, air conditioners and heaters failing, the chapter on maintenance will reveal some of the problems to anticipate when heading up a school. The maintenance staff also offers crucial services in the running of a school. The perceptive principal should anticipate the rough tides that might swell in that area. Being intuitive about the janitorial needs of the school contributes to the overall healthy atmosphere of the school. Also, responsiveness to the staff's needs makes for a better environment for the children and adults.

Building community and culture is the key to success for schools. The chapter on school culture will provide keys to climate control. School climate is a critical component in keeping students connected to school. It is also crucial in keeping teachers committed to their students. To maintain a healthy school environment, an intuitive leader must be able to check the waters, recognize stagnant cultures, and build positive school community.

Threats to the school community and safety can come in so many forms. From fire drills to lockdowns, school security must be ensured. No issue is more serious than that of school safety. School violence is a concern on every parent's mind. The growing concern of school violence will be discussed in the chapter on school safety along with suggestions for keeping students and staff safe and secure.

Other than school security, the next greatest fear on an administrator's mind may be that of a lawsuit. Educators must know and follow the law, but knowing what is legal and what is not can sometimes be very difficult to ascertain. From breaking up fights to dealing with access to records and confidentiality, this chapter will try to help the practical principal tow the line. Some examples of how administrators pushed past the legal limit will also be given.

Back in the day, school discipline appeared to be so cut and dried with very clear consequences for infractions. Most disciplinary matters are not as simple as dealing with a kindergartner who has relieved himself on the playground. The chapter on school discipline will include administrators' stories of some of the most unusual interactions regarding discipline that they have had with students. Classroom management will also be addressed along with some of the serious topics that school officials are dealing with today regarding school discipline.

Being a principal means that parents will often have unrealistic or expansive expectations of you. The practical principal knows that there is a difference in taking responsibility for what takes place on a school campus, and doing everything on the campus. Such a school leader does not have to carry the burden alone, and can call for reinforcement. From great expectations to realistic goals, the chapter entitled "The Buck Stops Here" will discuss how to communicate effectively with parents.

"Final Thoughts at the End of the Day" is the concluding chapter that will try to inspire the men and women who lead students successfully into the future. With over forty years of experience in public education between us, we appreciate the difficult task that administrators have. We thank these leaders who awe us everyday. We hope that we can remind them to take their sense of humor, tissue, and optimistic attitudes along with them on their journey.

Chapter Two

Staff: Help! The Lunch Ladies Are Fighting!

As we stated in our first chapter, the quality of the connections and bonds between your employees, teachers, parents, and students has a profound and direct impact on the accomplishment of the goals you hope to achieve together and, in a larger sense, the ultimate realization of the organization's mission and vision. When you and your staff share a common identity, a sense of community, and a deep connection to each other and what you've agreed to achieve together, you establish and maintain the facilitative conditions within which positive cooperative achievement and success can occur and flourish.

If you have a staff that works in isolation and has a poor quality of connection among all or most of the school stakeholders, cooperative and successful pursuit of commonly held goals becomes very difficult and hard to manage. This chapter will discuss how the practical principal can effectively attend to and deal with periodic and unexpected employee conflicts to diminish their negative effect on the quality of the bonds between stakeholders and the optimal level of achievement the organization can attain.

Many conflicts among employees center around the difference in their specific functions and, in some cases, educational differences, misunderstandings, differences in sensitivities, and sometimes, deliberate meanness on the part of one or more coworkers. In the early years of my career, I (Werner) was a member of an elementary faculty that I thought was the next best thing to my actual family. We celebrated happiness and sadness together and seemed united around the goal of doing what was absolutely best for children each and every day together. I believed the quality of our mutual connection was strong and indestructible. It's odd how a stray word here, or a senseless thought there, can completely demoralize a coworker whom the moment before seemed deeply connected to and happy with the person who uttered the offensive words.

One day, a teacher with about two and a half years of experience who was considerably younger than the instructional assistant who helped her daily, made a remark to the instructional assistant that she considered condescending and demeaning. They were having a conversation about an activity that they were planning together for the children. In the early stages of the conversation they were brainstorming and freely sharing ideas. After a few moments, they had a difference of opinion about one aspect of the activity. This simple difference of opinion became frustrating for both of them. At some point in the conversation, the teacher said, "We're just going to have to agree to disagree and do it my way." Then, without thinking, and probably without a lot of negative intent, the teacher said, "You know, I am the teacher and you are just an instructional assistant!"

Who would have thought two simple sentences could so completely create a schism between two classifications of coworkers for almost one-and-a-half months. The instructional assistant, feeling devalued and unappreciated, immediately left the teacher's classroom and went to the break room to console herself. While there she vented to another instructional assistant, who was equally appalled by the statement. You can imagine how over the next two days this simple two-sentence event spread like wildfire among the staff. Instructional assistants, who previously enjoyed great working relationships with their teachers, suddenly stopped using initiative and even diminished their cooperative spirits when engaged in work together. Some teachers, after hearing the teacher's point of view, felt that their instructional assistants were being petty and began treating them only a little better than children in their directives to them. What began as collegial, cooperative, and appreciative working relationships had deteriorated almost exponentially because of a lapse in human sensitivity. This incident even caused a rift between teachers.

Some felt the rookie teacher had made a silly blunder and should learn from her mistake by being immersed in its consequences. There were others who felt a little bit more superior, professionally, to instructional assistants and continued to reinforce the perception that instructional assistants were little more than worker bees at their beck and call. Of all people in the school, the principal was the last to know of the event. And he only found out when he noticed overt signs of anger and hostility between many of his teachers and instructional assistants. As a member of the instructional team, I knew about the faux pas within two hours of its occurrence.

A practical principal must possess a sixth sense concerning the emotional health and well-being of the school. He or she must know and be aware of the personalities of all coworkers, must be aware of and understand the importance of body language as an indicator of an individual's state of being, and must be mobile and visible throughout the school day to monitor the quality of instruction and stakeholder interactions. I can't help but think that if the teacher and the instructional assistant who had experienced the original problem shared a connection to and trusted in their principal, they may have been able to solve their problem together without disruptively affecting the rest of the staff. Thus, a school teacher must be perceived by all stakeholders as someone they can go to for assistance in a crisis without apprehension or fear of negative consequences. To diffuse the potentially destructive potential of an event, words, or interactions, the practical principal must be prepared to effectively address the problem in the earliest phase of the issue's development.

As the title of this chapter implies, conflict has the potential to impact any working group on campus, including the wonderful individuals who work so hard to prepare student meals everyday. One day, I (Deana) was called in to mediate a conflict between several food service workers. At first, I thought that the call for help was a joke. After all, one of the workers just poked her head into my office and said, "You better come quickly, before they come to blows! Jodi and Carol (names have been changed) are yelling at each other." When I looked up from the mounds of paperwork before me, I asked, "Who?" The emphatic reply told me that I was needed immediately.

Not a moment too soon, I walked into the food service office to find the women shouting at one other. Upon seeing me, they lowered their voices and allowed me to speak. The situation was tense, but I was able to ascertain that the argument began over fairness in workload. Luckily, the disagreement was resolved without physical contact and lunch was served on time that day.

Unfortunately, workload disputes among coworkers are rather commonplace. Teachers especially feel overworked, so if class sizes do not match the make-up of the students within the classroom (e.g., how many students need special services, etc.), then those educators may become very disillusioned, angry, and resentful. Sometimes, two colleagues of equal stature can become so disappointed in or suspicious of one another that it disrupts their working relationship and adversely impacts the school's performance itself. A case in point is illustrated by a situation in which the only two teachers on the same grade level (fifth grade) nearly came to blows over the difference in their class sizes and who was receiving perceived preferential treatment from the principal. The situation had actually been created and ultimately reinforced by the school principal's actions.

An age-old issue between teachers as far back as many can remember has been the notion that one teacher always gets the best kids and another teacher is always stuck with the more challenging students. In this case, the principal had two veteran teachers, one male and one female, teaching his fifth-grade students. When the year began, the female teacher came to him and said, "I'd like to have the highest reading group and all gifted students on my grade level placed in my class this year to see how far I can take them." The principal, who valued great scores on district standardized tests, was intrigued by the idea that his best students could possibly achieve better than they ever had before if he granted the teacher's request. Not thinking of discussing this issue with both teachers present and formalizing a plan that both agreed with, the principal simply agreed to the teacher's request and divided both classes accordingly. The second teacher, clueless as to what had happened, was starting the year with about the same number of students as the female teacher.

At the school, the office staff tried to maintain class sizes at each grade level to be equal. When a new student enrolled on a grade level they would give the student to the class that had fewer students. If they had an equal amount, the person who got the last student was passed over and the student would be given to another teacher. When the next new student enrolled, the next teacher with a lower number of students would get the student. Within a few days, the male teacher noticed that as new students arrived on his grade level he appeared to get the new student each time. Without talking to anyone else, he started to count each student that went into the other teacher's class in the mornings to compare their class sizes. Being a veteran he didn't want to jump to any conclusions before he discussed a perceived anomaly with others. By the end of the third week of school, he believed he had four more students assigned to him than the other teacher.

When he asked the other teacher about it, she said that she had a few people absent and a couple of them would be chronic attendance problems this year. What the male teacher didn't know was that when the principal agreed to implement the female teacher's idea, he also capped her class so it would never exceed twenty-five students. He felt that by capping the class, the female teacher would have the best opportunity to provide instruction that would most optimally address the students' potentials each and every day. Once the male teacher was convinced he had five more students than the other teacher, the two teachers became hostile toward one another. It got so bad that they would not even allow their students to interact with each other on the playground.

These particular teachers even requested that the classes be separated at lunch and placed on opposite sides of the lunchroom. The male teacher made up his mind that the principal had picked a favorite in the other teacher and given her a "dream class," while giving him all the rest. He didn't feel comfortable talking to the principal about it because the principal rarely, if ever, spoke to him. In his class he had several children with disciplinary issues, had less positive qualitative parental support, and had the most instructionally challenged students in the grade level assigned to him. With each passing day, his attitude, his commitment to his students, and his connection to his colleague deteriorated.

Although his class had the most transience of the two classes, he consistently had twenty-nine students or more in attendance in his class daily throughout the year. The other teacher's class never exceed twenty-five students and, at one time, got as low as twenty-one students. When March came around the students participated in their annual standardized testing program. Although the students in the female teacher's class scored high on their test battery as a class, they did not score to the heightened expectations of the teacher and principal. Likewise, the male teacher students' class achievement on their test battery was extraordinarily low. The school's combined grade-level achievement for that year was significantly lower than it had been for three consecutive years prior.

The practical principal should never intentionally set up instructional assignments which appear one-sided, unfair, or smack of favoritism. The well-prepared principal, when considering innovation and different instructional arrangements within the school, should plan such changes with all relevant stakeholders who may be affected by the change. By including relevant stakeholders in the dialog about planning potential instructional change or structural change, the practical principal can build consensus and "buy in" among stakeholders, which will make success possible. This proactive and involved approach will also enhance the school's culture and commitment to the goals and innovations it strives to achieve while avoiding the negative impacts that were experienced in the case above.

The educational leaders seeking to establish a cohesive and cooperative school culture must necessarily focus on and be attentive to a myriad of human factors. The practical principal must expect, nurture, and model the human values of the worth and dignity of each and every individual within the school. He or she must communicate, celebrate, and articulate the unique importance of every individual in their role within the school to and for all others within the school. From the custodians to the food service workers, from the teacher's assistant to teachers themselves, and from the office staff to the other school support personnel (counselors, media specialists, special area teachers, visiting support staff, speech/language therapists), the practical principal must validate the mutual interdependence and importance of every stakeholder within the school.

In so doing, the new principal will enhance the school's ability to create and establish a school culture that values the respective positive contributions of every individual while building the capacity to create long-lasting and effective bonds between all of the school's stakeholders. Initial and focused attention to building effective bonds among stakeholders will ensure that those bonds are extended to the students, their parents, and their families. This focus will also enable the same effective bonds to be established between the school in its community, between volunteers and the school, and between the school itself and the district's administration.

Even when stakeholders share a highly positive, qualitative bond and a single-minded commitment to their combined goals, much effort and attentiveness should be focused toward the quality of their connectedness. Something as simple as incentive money can pit stakeholders against one another and undermine an otherwise successful staff's commitment to their goals and each other. Throughout the nation today, schools are ever-focused on accountability for enhanced student achievement and instructional effectiveness. Virtually every state, in some way or fashion, grades each school annually on its instructional accomplishments. A school's success or failure hinges primarily upon the aggregate growth of its students as evidenced on standardized test achievement. Imposed federal standards to demonstrate "adequate progress" annually across all demographic subgroups places great pressure upon every school's stakeholders to prove that their school is adequately meeting the needs of every student within it.

In some states, teachers are rewarded individually with "pay for performance" incentives based upon the aggregate growth of students assigned to them. In other states, schools are rewarded with incentive funds for aggregate student growth school wide. Four times in my career, I (Werner) have been either blessed or cursed with the responsibility of helping a school divide incentive money awarded in recognition of improved aggregate student performance. On each occasion, given there was a limited amount to be distributed, the schools were charged with developing a distribution that they felt was fair and appropriate. Of course, during these times, great care was taken to have discussions with all stakeholders within each school's professional community about the amount available and ideas for how it was to be shared equitably.

Typically, one argument always surfaced: that those who did the teaching should benefit the most from the incentive money. Then, the group deemed next most contributory to the success of student performance would get the next level of distribution, and so on until the money was completely divided. In most cases, the more directly you are involved in instruction, it was reasoned, the larger your respective individual award should be. Others argued that if the classrooms were not properly prepared each day, the learning environment would not be conducive to effective learning. Yet others argued that if the students weren't properly fed in the mornings and at lunch time they could not focus on their studies, and therefore would not retain any of the instruction they were provided. You can kind of see where this is going.

All of these arguments came up every single time a school in which I was principal received an incentive reward. The difficulty facing a caring principal during such times is that all stakeholders must feel they participated in a process that fairly considered and rewarded everyone's relative contribution toward the school's success. In my case, in the four times my schools received incentive money, the distribution was different each time. Every time one of my schools received incentive money, all stakeholders were engaged in conversations about how to fairly distribute the funds prior to actually distributing the funds.

Three of these times occurred at the same school over a four-year period. Each discussion focused on different issues and different needs salient to the school and its staff for the school year in question. In one case, over half of the funds received were unanimously approved by the stakeholders to upgrade the school's computer lab with the remainder of the funds being equally distributed among every employee within the school. In other cases, award amounts vary according to criteria agreed upon by all stakeholders prior to distribution.

The key to success here was a dialog that provided ample consideration of all stakeholders' input in decisions that promised to have significant impact on the school's learning community and its culture. I know of schools that have been adversely impacted and experienced frustration, disappointment, and divisiveness because such decisions were arbitrarily determined by a few in favor of only a few at the apparent expense and neglect of the validation of the efforts of others. The pragmatic principal will be wise to consider the myriad of factors which may pose a threat to the collegiality and cohesiveness of the school's staff whenever compensation monetary or otherwise is an issue at the forefront.

Before concluding, we want to touch on the importance of staff trust. While school leaders rely on educators to make responsible decisions, especially those that directly affect students, the practical principal must be counterintuitive when it comes to anticipating potential problems involving both groups. One case in point involves two classes of kindergartners who took a field trip to the small, local airport.

The trip, in and of itself, appeared to be entirely educational and appropriate. The young students would learn about the workings of an airport and have the opportunity to view an airplane up close. The school administrator thought that the field trip would entail just that and, perhaps, a stop to get ice cream before returning to school. The trip, however, veered from the expected to the totally unexpected quite rapidly.

What occurred during that infamous and true airport field trip could have proven disastrous and even fatal; luckily no one was injured, except the trust level of teachers from then on. In touring the paraloft at the airport, the two kindergarten teachers were asked by the parachute training staff if they were interested in free tandem jump lessons. The teachers readily seized upon the opportunity to demonstrate to their students what a parachute jump would be like. If the lesson had stopped there, the trip still could have been successful.

Following the training session, though, the teachers were asked if they were interested in actually taking a tandem jump from a plane. Without thinking, the young teachers agreed to do so, left their students with adult chaperones, and proceeded to parachute out of the sky. If the teachers had thought for a moment about the potential consequences of their actions, one would hope that they would not have taken that flight. Luckily, no one was injured, but how devastated would those children have been if they had seen one or both of their teachers drop to their death?

From an administrator's point of view, the dramatic impact on the students, alone, would be cause for consternation. Potential liabilities would also have come into play as well as the psychological repercussions. The administrator was not advised of the occurrences on the trip, but heard about it from discussions that were being held in the faculty workroom. The practical principal is a good listener and one who learns to anticipate all the potential actions and missteps that staff might make.

In conclusion, orchestrating a group effort toward achieving short- or long-term common goals requires an enormous amount of human relations skills. It assumes that within an organization's core culture, common values, a common mission, and an overriding vision is shared and valued by all stakeholders. With this common interest as its base, a school can build around that base a single and effective school culture, which will allow it to achieve to its highest potential level instructionally and as an organizational unit.

Although today's principals are thought of as instructional leaders and visionaries, they are still expected to manage their schools effectively. To be effective, the practical principal must not only be a visionary leader, but must also know how to effectively manage and nurture the human relationships within the school. Through this delicate balance and blending of leadership and management, the practical principal can guide the school and its staff toward maintaining the highest quality of interactive relationships while striving to accomplish all the goals they expect to achieve together.

Chapter Three

Substitutes:
Tell Me the Sub Didn't Say That

Although a chapter on staffing is already included, Werner and I both feel that the topic of substitute teachers deserves a section unto itself. In spite of the fact that this section will be somewhat brief compared to other chapters, we want to underscore the importance of taking a serious look at the substitutes on campus. The practical principal, despite (hopefully) not being in charge of calling the substitutes him- or herself, must be knowledgeable about the individuals supervising the students while the primary teacher is away. Whether it is just for one day or a few weeks, an ineffective sub can wreak havoc on the internal workings of the school. No kidding!

Substitute teachers can be a Godsend or a nightmare depending on who steps into that role. Ideally, the substitute would be a retired, certified teacher willing to take the helm at a moment's notice. Realistically, the teachers have to take who they can get to cover their classes for the duration of their absence from school. Despite having passed criminal background checks, some substitute teachers have no prior experience with the population they seek to serve. What we mean is that some individuals who solicit work as substitutes seem to lack the desire, insight, or ability to work with the student population, or children at all.

Of course, many of us have heard the news reports about the extreme behaviors of substitutes, and teachers, for that matter. Certainly, a no-nonsense principal must quickly and decisively deal with those issues. We have no desire to make light of circumstances that involve harm or putting the students in danger in any way. The less extreme, but rather seemingly improbable, behaviors are those that the practical principal must also be prepared to deal with.

For instance, one substitute teacher, while not in violation of the dress code since she was not a lead teacher, wore blue jeans to work. That type of dress per se does not necessarily present a problem, although some might say it lacks professionalism, which is an argument that need not be delved into at this time. This particular substitute had visible tattoos, though, just above the waistline of her blue jeans so that when she extended to write on the board, the entire class could view the artwork. Not so hard for a practical principal to deal with, you might say. Well, try dealing with parents who complained about their child seeing a snake going into the back of a substitute's pants!

Another incident involving the apparel of substitutes includes not only being sensitive to body-size issues, but handling matters that involve the opposite sex. One rather unusual set of circumstances involved a very overweight substitute who was wearing all white. The weight of the substitute was not a complicating factor. This particular sub was very competent and able to function perfectly in the role of a substitute teacher. Her undergarment, though not visible from behind, was quite discernible in the front. She had chosen to wear a red thong underneath her white dress.

The practical principal must be able to seek assistance when necessary. In the above scenario, which is another true story by the way, the principal sought out a same-sex colleague to address the matter with the substitute. No offense was taken and to the administrator's knowledge, no further problems were encountered with this otherwise capable substitute.

The insightful principal must also be ready to address situations that involve less than due diligence on the part of the substitute teacher. My seventeen-year-old son shared this incident with me (Deana). His substitute fell asleep in class during a movie. When the movie ended, the substitute did not stir, allowing time for students to get their cell phones out and document the entire scene with the video and camera capabilities on their phones. Among the shots that the students took was the drool coming out of the sleeping substitute's mouth. It did not take long for those images to reach the Internet via YouTube. Such images are not ones that a practical principal would want to project to parents and the community at large.

Knowing the experience that a substitute might bring into the school is always helpful to a new principal. A limited history with children is never a good sign. The well-trained principal can spot those substitutes, oftentimes with a glazed look in their eyes, simply by walking down the hall. Such a principal is ubiquitous, or omnipresent, thereby very aware of the din and disruption coming from the room inhabited by students and one lone, inexperienced substitute.

Only one hour into the school day, I (Deana) had a substitute come into the guidance office, burst into tears, and summarily announce that she could not handle the class and was going home. After attempting to appease her to no avail, I quickly had to jump in and supervise the special education students. In the meantime, the seasoned principal, with help I might add, searched for someone to supervise the students for the entire day. Another area that could prove to be deleterious to the effective functioning of the school and to the educational process involves the communication skills of the substitute teacher. We are not referring to the wonderful use of alliteration, metaphors, or even unintelligible speech patterns, rather it is the inappropriate interchange of thoughts, opinions, or information that often prove to be more worrisome and disconcerting.

The well-versed principal does not want to be put in a position of having to explain to parents why the substitute thought it was acceptable to write C-R-A-P on the board and then proceed to use descriptive terminology about the use of the word. This incident actually occurred at a middle school, much to the chagrin of the school administrators. Other troublesome forms of communication include the use of cell phones during class, utilizing the Internet to find a date, or assorted various glaring violations that one would not expect from an individual in a supervisory role of children.

The practical principal can guard against distressing situations involving substitutes by preparing these adults ahead of time as to what the expectations of them are. Most systems have an approved list of substitutes and those lists need to be routinely culled in an effort to prevent further mishaps from occurring. Substitute training at the beginning of the year can also prove valuable.

At the end of the school day, a practical principal does not want to be caught holding head in hands wondering why in the world that adult was ever allowed on the campus. Mistakes do happen, but the most prepared administrator must be hypervigilant about protecting children and their right to an education. The success of the school can be dependent on the school leadership. The practical principal keeps that success and student safety at the forefront of his or her mind.

Chapter Four

Counselors:
Does the Counselor Need Counseling?

Guidance counselors, reading coaches, curriculum specialists, media specialists, and other certified instructional support personnel provide crucial services for students, parents, and staff members that are vitally essential to the ultimate accomplishment of the mission and goals of the school's learning community. In a best-case scenario, these highly specialized personnel can be informal leaders within the organization, supporting cohesion, collegiality, and instructional efficacy within the learning community, or they can be divisive elements within a staff that can impede progress toward the common goals of the organization.

As a counselor, I (Deana) think it is important to isolate and examine the role of the school counselor. I do not intend to diminish the importance of the other specialists on the school grounds, but both Werner and I have school counseling backgrounds. Those backgrounds stem from a deep desire to help meet the needs of children and their families. The unique value of a school counselor should not be overlooked, yet the counselors' plates are full, and everyone (from staff to parents) continues to expect more and more from them.

From counseling students to scheduling and everything in between, the stress can be overwhelming, even for sage counselors. This chapter will explore how to get the best from your counselor without pushing that individual over the edge. Reading coaches and media specialists can be included in this mix. Although I have known other professionals to cry out in despair, I also must admit that I (Deana) am one of those counselors who has cried to and in front of her principal (unfortunately, I have also cried in front of colleagues and teachers, too) more than once. I am not proud of my tearful interactions, but am ready to admit it to underscore the growing burden that counselors must carry.

The paperwork alone can bury the counselor, so that person cannot even think about coming out from under it to, dare we say, counsel students. Counseling students in an effort to help them achieve academic success, social competence, and emotional well-being should be the focus of every school counseling program. The reality is, however, that the counselor's time can be usurped by the bureaucratic red tape of academia. The risk is that the counselor becomes no more than an overpaid secretary—a common lament from those counselors who understand what a difference they could make if allowed to do so.

The practical principal must have a counselor who is an effective time manager and who can keep on an even keel temperamentally. While it is true being calmer about situations can certainly help counselors deal with situations more effectively, those of us who are a bit more high-strung also have value. The counselor's job may include making home visits when parents or students cannot be reached. The home visits alone can be enough to send any counselor over the edge, yet that individual must cope calmly and coolly with whatever comes up on the excursions.

One dilemma that I have encountered that has proved problematic for me over the years in my role as counselor is that I tend to laugh when I get nervous. It is something that frequently happens on trips into the unknown—I am referring to home visits. From talking to parents about a student's glasses while spying a hatchet on the counter (no lie, it really happened), to talking loudly to a grandparent to mistakenly compensate for her blindness, home visits are one-of-a-kind experiences.

Other home visit occurrences that I have experienced have been more troubling than humorous, but no less anxiety-ridden for me. Treading carefully through the waste of more than ten dogs in the home and finding dirty diapers and trash in the corners of the rooms where children slept is one such example. Wondering whether the strong ammonia-like odor coming from the mobile home was crystal meth being cooked up and how the students' lives would be affected, or whether the trailer would blow up, was another.

These adventures, or ordeals, as some may describe them, serve to remind the counselor and knowing principal about the significant role that can be played by the person in that position. The events, however, can also overwhelm the individual with guilt when the people-person is bogged down in paperwork. It is a balancing act that the counselor must learn to do well.

The effective leader should be able to readily identify the strengths and weakness in the counseling program. Using such identification as a tool to implement strategies to improve the program, the counselor may serve as one of the school's (and the students') greatest assets. The counselor can help foster community among the staff, increase parent involvement, boost student achievement, and build strong relationships with the students. At his worst, though, the counselor may become disheartened, bitter, disillusioned, and not useful to anyone.

The attuned principal can help remedy a counselor's waning self-confidence by remaining acutely aware of just how expansive and important the counselor's job is. The counselor's ultimate goal is to help students achieve at or above their ability levels, be emotionally healthy, socially competent, and able to make decisions about their future after graduation. Other than a teacher, what more important staff member can make as much of an impact as the counselor? Okay, I know that I am biased, but really, what position is more vital on a school campus (excluding educators and cafeteria workers—food is of vast importance, especially for students whose primary meals of the day are at school)?

A practical principal knows that for the learning community to effectively work toward the achievement of its vision and mission, every stakeholder must be committed to and believe in the stated goals they commonly share. When each of these specialized stakeholders truly understands and embraces their roles relative to the stated goals and objectives of the learning community, they can provide invaluable support to classroom teachers and their students. Such support can reinforce and enhance their cooperative efforts to provide optimal educational opportunities and instruction for every student in the school.

It would not be unfair to say that the ultimate dream of the principal is very much like that of a professional football coach. The professional football coach strives to orchestrate the combined efforts of a diverse, highly specialized group of individuals, organized as a team to achieve the ultimate goal of winning the national championship. Of course, the coach aims to have the best players for each position. Simply having the best players, though, does not guarantee that the team will win the Super Bowl.

The wise coach knows, as does the practical principal, whether it is the superstar and journeyman or the prima donna and the utility player, each has a vitally important role to play in the organization's success. Like a professional coach, the practical principal must decide whether to call every play or to rely on the expertise of the specialized members of the team to help guide cooperative decision making to achieve success. The remainder of this chapter will examine this question in greater detail to hopefully provide insights that can be used by the practical principal in guiding the combined efforts of specialists, teachers, students, and all other stakeholders in striving to achieve the best outcomes they can possibly achieve together. Throughout this book, the reader will find situations and events discussed from both a counselor's and a principal's perspective that will illustrate the juxtaposition of their roles and responsibilities as they relate to particular issues.

Very rarely does a principal have the opportunity to open a brand-new school and select every staff member before it opens. Most principals are selected and assigned to an existing school with an existing staff. The teachers, support workers, and special-area teachers assigned to the school have probably been an organizational unit together for quite some time prior to the new principal's assignment to that school. Given they have shared an interactive dynamic for, in many cases, years before the principal has arrived, the developmental task facing the principal is to study and understand that dynamic, the shared history of that organizational unit, and the previous accomplishments or lack thereof of that organizational unit. It is not unusual for a principal to be assigned to a school that has met with limited success over the years and has little or no cohesion among its stakeholders.

In such schools, staff members typically engage in what can be commonly referred to as "parallel play." As hard as each individual tries to perform their function at the highest level possible, without shared goals, effective leadership, and appropriate facilitation, very little organizational success can be achieved. Even when each individual is highly qualified, conscientious, and caring, without effective leadership, motivation, validation, and effective articulation, very little aggregate progress can be made toward the stated goals of the school.

When a new principal is assigned to this kind of school, there is enormous potential for growth as a learning community, for the establishment of an effective school climate and culture, and for growth in aggregate student performance that can be reinforced and replicated year after year. To make these things happen, the practical principal must explore the internal "politics" and "informal leadership" of the school to gain a sense of perspective about what must be done to facilitate the growth and development of the learning community to more effectively address and meet the needs of its students.

A case in point is illustrated by my last assignment as a principal several years ago. After twenty-two years of service at a previous school, the superintendent called me (Werner) into his office to let me know he was transferring me to another school for the next school year. He prefaced his conversation with me by saying he was proud of the accomplishments I was able to make at my previous school. He further stated that the school that I would be assigned to for the next year had been stagnant in its performance for a number of years.

The superintendent believed that while it had a demographically challenged student population, a lot of potential existed for the school to become a high-performing learning community. As attached as I was to my previous school, I embraced the superintendent's vote of confidence and prepared to begin my assignment. I was notified of this change in June and therefore had approximately two months to study the demographics of the school, staff dynamics, and its student performance history. In my research, I found that although the majority of the staff possessed the skills and abilities necessary to become high-performing, the staff seemed out of touch with its potentials.

The school's curriculum was fragmented and poorly articulated across grade levels and the staff did not share a sense of cohesion and mutual acceptance consistent with that of the single school culture. Aggregate student performance seemed to have flatlined at a level of mediocrity beneath that of the perceived abilities of the students, faculty, and staff. The school was absolutely ripe for positive change and organizational refocus. For years, each of its classroom teachers had taken the curriculum provided them and worked with their students in apparent instructional isolation from all other teachers. Although all staff members were extremely professional and competent, they performed their various functions as discrete units without specific and focused instructional direction.

The guidance counselor performed services for all stakeholders who solicited her help. The media specialists provided the appropriate media, equipment, and resources for teachers to enhance their instructional efforts, and the curriculum specialist provided classroom teachers with instructional materials to assist and enhance their daily efforts. Each of these support professionals were also informal leaders in their own right. Yet without appropriate direction and focus, their leadership skills that could enhance the organization's progress toward commonly held goals were largely untapped.

In such a school culture, even when progress is possible, it can be severely limited due to a lack of direction, guidance, and successful focus upon the overriding vision and mission of the school. As the school's new principal, I felt it was important to redefine its identity, its vision and mission, and reestablish a school culture that was conducive to and focused upon its future growth as a learning community. Together we selected appropriate curricula responsive to the needs of our learning community. We redefined our operational vision and mission and, through a series of discussions, developed a plan to improve and articulate instruction throughout and across our grade levels.

We sought and obtained "buy in" from all stakeholders in the goals and directions we set out to pursue together. We obtained a commitment to long-term staff training, which included all appropriate stakeholders, in an effort to improve instruction and instructional support schoolwide. Finally, we selected and developed a school-based leadership team (many of which were existing informal leaders) that not only assisted in guiding the efforts of the members of each instructional subgroup, but also capitalized upon the leadership abilities of specialized teachers to effectively support our progress toward our commonly held goals. Of course this is a simplification of a process that took a considerable amount of time. Cohesiveness, mutual cooperation, and a single school culture did not emerge overnight. It did, however, occur in positive incremental steps over time.

In our first year together, we were most successful in developing a single-minded identity as a learning community. Our student performance aggregately improved about 15 percent over the previous year. Along the way, we experienced growing pains and barriers to progress, some internal and some external to the school. The key to success, regardless of the barriers and growing pains we experienced, was the effective nurturing of working relationships among the staff guided by the informal and formal leadership team in the school. In sharing adversity and growth together, a learning community evolved centered on a commonly held and cherished mission and the notion that we together could achieve what previously was considered improbable and had yet to be accomplished in the school's eight-year history.

Florida has a school grading system that rates schools on a scale of from "A" to "F." The school had for the four years prior received a grade of "C" for their efforts. By the end of our first year together, the school again had achieved a letter grade of "C," but it had improved over the previous year to within two points of a "B." With additional training and focus, by the end of our second year we jumped two letter grades and received a school grade of "A" from the state Department of Education. In successive years, the school's learning community continued to show sustained and ongoing growth and progress.

Over the next three years, the school sustained and was awarded grades reflecting high-performing aggregate student achievement. The school's climate and culture continued to grow to meet its highest potential and the needs of its students. Within a five-year period, the school successfully redefined its position within the district from seventh place out of ten schools in its first year under a new principal to number one in student achievement among elementary schools in the district in its fifth year.

In addition to achieving the highest school grade awarded by the state for three of five years, in its fifth year under new leadership, the school achieved "Adequate Progress" in meeting federal "No Child Left Behind" performance criteria across all subgroups within the school and a school grade of an "A." To place this achievement in context, the school's demographic profile showed its population had one of the three highest poverty rates within the district, had one of the highest exceptional student education population rates within the district, and had the fourth highest minority population rates within the district. In its fifth year as a redefined, rededicated learning community, the school had outperformed all other elementary schools within the district.

Success can and will be achieved when a learning community establishes a single school culture, when it optimizes the abilities and potentials of every stakeholder within it toward their commonly shared and held goals, and when it utilizes all of its formal and informal leaders effectively to facilitate their combined efforts together. As was stated earlier, it would be an extreme luxury for a principal to open up a new school and be able to select every member of the school staff with the goal in mind of only selecting the best of the best. Yet from time to time, a principal will be able to select one or more of those highly specialized staff members such as counselors, reading coaches, curriculum specialists, media specialists, and other support specialists, thereby affording them the opportunity to enhance the learning community and grow performance capacity within the school.

When making these choices, the principal will occasionally have existing staff members who have obtained additional certifications or specializations apply for these positions. The practical principal, on these occasions, would be wise to take into consideration and understand the internal politics of the school. The practical principal should review the personal power of such applicants among the staff, the objectivity of the applicant, allegiance to or conflict with individuals or groups within the school, and past performance and track record in their current capacities in doing what is best for children. The practical principal will also realize that many times these specialized personnel are often between "a rock and a hard place." When it comes to parents and teachers, students and teachers, and staff and administration, conflicting views and opinions often complicate cooperative efforts to solve problems.

With this knowledge the practical principal will establish selection criteria that recognizes that the desired capabilities of these specialized professionals should include diplomacy, sensitivity, a team spirit, an intense focus upon the common good of the learning community, and an ability to be a moderating influence in the face of difficulty, challenge, or impending change. These individuals are essential to the maintenance of cohesion and cooperation among the staff and all stakeholders in the learning community. They can and often do solve problems in their earliest stages, which could, if left unaddressed and allowed to fester, compromise the effective movement of the school toward its commonly held goals.

Their role in supporting and nurturing the positive movement of all stakeholders toward these goals is a priceless asset to the school and the principal. In an ideal situation, the practical principal may have a faculty and staff that is self actualized. At its best, such a school will not require much intervention from the principal at all, because every stakeholder is not only aware of, but also embraces their respective role in contributing to the success of the school. Such schools are capable of and practice a democratic leadership process wherein every stakeholder participates in the optimal development of the instructional programs and processes they seek to effectively implement together.

Through collegiality and cooperative development, schools that exhibit the readiness to do so under the right leadership will exhibit and sustain the highest level of performance among all staff members and embrace continuous quality improvement. The practical principal must be able to identify what stage of leadership development and readiness the staff exhibits. Likewise, the practical principal must have an ability to accept the level of leadership development and readiness the school exhibits to understand which leadership skills must be expressed and exhibited by the principal to assist the school in moving toward this democratic ideal.

The practical principal must not only have skills in personality and performance assessment, but should also possess an eclectic understanding of a variety of leadership styles to be able to match appropriate leadership with emergent needs to effectively facilitate positive growth within the learning community. The practical principal must also identify and understand potential barriers to the continuous growth and sustained success of the organization. With this knowledge, the practical principal can utilize the specific skills of their specialized personnel and their respective leadership abilities to effectively address and overcome these barriers to growth and success.

In conclusion, if the school's media specialist treats the media and equipment housed in the media center as sacred treasures that must last forever, they may very well not allow these media to be used toward the benefit of the students and teachers in the classroom. If the guidance counselor is delegated miscellaneous and unrelated administrative duties, while not being allowed to meet the needs of individual or small groups of children and teachers, positive student performance can be adversely impacted. When a reading coach or curriculum specialist is required to spend all their time managing instructional materials instead of providing mentoring and classroom instructional support, classroom teachers may fall short of their instructional goals. The practical principal must truly understand the interactive dynamics of all stakeholders within the school, must understand their historical roles and their past practices, and must successfully articulate the future direction and mission of the school.

Integral to the school's success, the practical principal must be visible, approachable, and involved. The practical principal must surely understand that the optimal accomplishment and achievements attributable to the school spring from the combined efforts of everyone who works directly with the children in their specific and focused capacities each and every day. What is accomplished by the school, its students, and all of its stakeholders is directly related to the quality of their combined efforts. Guidance counselors, media specialists, reading coaches, curriculum specialists, and all other specialized support personnel can significantly contribute to quality of the achievements that can be accomplished within and by the students and staff.

The extent and quality of their connection to all other stakeholders within the school and the goals they commonly share will determine and define the ultimate success of the school's ability to meet and exceed its mission and vision as a learning community. Given these final thoughts, the innovative principal will enhance and improve the school's potential for positive growth and organizational success when the efforts of the specialized personnel are effectively recognized, developed, and integrated with the combined efforts of all stakeholders within the learning community.

Chapter Five

Assistant Principals: Second in Command

It has been said that the position of a school administrator is one of the loneliest positions in the school. By nature of the responsibilities and authority incumbent upon an administrator, there are very few, if any, school personnel in whom an administrator can confide. The administrator lacks someone to discuss confidential issues with and seek reinforcement from. Very few individuals are available on campus to glean advice from about decisions while making the hard choices incumbent upon the school's chief executive officer on a daily basis.

Some school principals are assigned to schools in which they have little or no administrative support. In these schools, the principal has sole responsibility and authority for all decisions and must deal with the business of the school in isolation, and at times, uncertainty. Usually, these schools have small student enrollments and a corresponding limited budget that precludes additional administrative support. Most schools, however, whether they are elementary or secondary, are staffed with an assistant principal. For the principal who knows how to effectively utilize them, an assistant principal can be one of the greatest assets available to the school.

In the best situation, an assistant principal can be a confidante to the principal, and thereby be an effective sounding board in the decision-making process for the school. This type of assistant can be of immense value as a source of professional, collegial, and leadership support for the school's principal. A skilled assistant principal can be a unifying influence among staff members, an instructional leader in every aspect of curricular development, and an excellent source of support to parents and students. The assistant principal can be of immense value as a liaison between the school and the community, the school and district support personnel, as well as between the school and local, state, or federal governmental entity representatives.

In some rare situations, an assistant principal can be an additional challenge for the principal striving to create and maintain a high performing, cohesive, and cooperative learning community. This chapter will explore issues surrounding the selection of assistant principals, along with issues concerning the school-based training and inclusion of assistant principals in the day-to-day operation of the school. This chapter will also provide suggestions for how a principal and assistant principal can blend their responsibilities and talents to create a high-performing administrative team for the school.

For most school systems, the pathway to a principalship usually includes at least a three-year placement as an assistant principal. Traditionally, minimal requirements for selection as an assistant principal include three or more years experience as a school-based teacher, and graduation from an accredited Master's-level educational leadership program. A candidate for an assistant principal position is typically required to have a passing score on the state's educational leadership certification examination, and a current and valid state license or certificate covering the area of educational leadership, school administration, and/or School Principal.

From state to state, these requirements may vary slightly, but generally include many of the same components. Most school systems view the position of assistant principal as a training position that is designed to prepare an assistant principal with the real-world background knowledge and experiences necessary to assume a school's primary leadership role in the future. The quality and quantity of the training received by an assistant principal under the tutelage of a principal varies according to the training abilities of the principal and the formalized administrator training processes/programs of the school system.

School-based administrators typically engage in two primary administrative activities on a daily basis, namely that of "leadership and management." Management is the activity most people consider the primary role of the school-based administrator. A variety of duties may be found under the umbrella of management. Those functions often include such routine tasks as scheduling, budgeting, maintaining and keeping inventory of all materials and equipment, student discipline, and supervisory duties of students and personnel. Additional duties involve teacher observations, program coordination, employee evaluations, and interviewing and hiring the school's employees (from food-service workers to instructional assistants to custodians to certified teaching and support personnel). Of course, an assistant principal is also called upon to assume what is usually referred to in the last line of most people's job description, "other duties as assigned by the principal, supervisor, or Superintendent."

Management activities are primarily concerned with monitoring and effectively tending to all aspects of the day-to-day operation of the school. Skill at these functions can usually be acquired in school-based training and from routine feedback provided by the principal throughout the course of the school year. In most cases, the training tends to resemble a mentor/mentee relationship wherein, through modeling and shadowing, the principal and assistant principal discuss conducting the daily business of the school on a routine basis. As issues, concerns, and situations emerge, opportunities for administrative growth, development, and applications of skills learned are provided for the assistant principal by the principal.

Additionally, some districts actually offer administrator development programs that address common duties and provide instruction on district approved process and policy implementation. This formalized and informal training process aids the assistant principal in becoming an effective school "manager" in preparation for dealing with issues and concerns as they arise on a daily basis even in the absence of the principal.

The second and more abstract of the activities engaged in by school administrators involves school leadership. Leadership activities include visioning and ongoing quality improvement. The administrators are also continually renewing their commitment to the mission of the learning communities. They do so through research and the development of an effective curriculum that addresses the learning needs of the entire school population. These activities tend to be among the highest order of activities in which administrators engage.

The goal of leadership activities is to create an optimal learning community that is responsive to the needs of its learners, ever focused on the real-world constraints of today (i.e., state and federal guidelines, demographic challenges, and other issues from external sources that may impact the school's day-to-day operation or goal achievement). The school leader must also consider impending changes that may impact the school well into the future. The practical principal will offer leadership training through the mentor/mentee relationship, and professional development including reading materials, conferences, and other training opportunities.

The practical principal will agree that the primary role of an assistant principal is that of a daily site manager. Although an assistant principal can be a school leader and can perform leadership functions, for the most part, that individual is involved in the nuts and bolts of the school's daily operation, reserving the leadership function for the school principal. The assistant principal is the day-to-day "firefighter" who deals with the school's emergent issues and crises. The prudent principal helps the assistant deal with the critical nature of this responsibility by being available for focused and recurring training and dialogue. Such opportunities will reinforce leadership to ensure the holistic development of the capabilities of the assistant principal. The optimal development of the assistant principal's capabilities and skills are an essential responsibility of the school principal.

The practical principal will help the assistant hone the skills necessary to lead a school. In worst-case scenarios, the assistant principal must develop competence in this area on his own through external sources. With twenty-one years of administrative experience, eleven of which have been at the principal level, I (Werner) have had the opportunity to serve with seven different assistant principals under my leadership. Since most principals spend a fair amount of time as assistant principals, they have a pretty good idea of the skills and capabilities they would like to see in an assistant principal serving under them.

If a principal considers him- or herself to have been an effective assistant principal, his or her own experiences and capabilities become a model for hiring an assistant. In my first assignment as a principal, I felt it was important to provide the best training possible for every assistant principal assigned to my administrative team. From my earliest days as a principal, I found utilizing the mentor/mentee approach to training most effective for my own leadership style. Daily dialogue and situational analysis was also emphasized and became the most useful approach for my teaching personality.

I used this approach quite effectively with two assistant principals over the period of six years. It continued to be an approach I was able to effectively use with all but three of the assistant principals who served under me. On three of the seven occasions, I received a new assistant principal wherein I was an active participant in the selection process. On four occasions, however, assistant principals were assigned to me as transfers from previous schools and prior administrative assignments.

Assistant principals were screened and selected by this particular system through a district-approved process identifying three potential candidates for the site principal to interview along with a selection committee. As stated earlier, three of my previous assistant principals were selected through this process. The practical principal embraces the opportunity to select all support personnel up to and including an assistant principal. The new hire may possess a host of unique qualities that vary from his or her predecessor, requiring a change in the division of responsibilities between the principal and assistant principal. The practical principal uses such changes to capitalize upon the strengths of both administrators while being cognizant of the areas that may be more challenging for the administrative team.

Much like the inherent differences among schools and student populations, intrinsic differences exist in the strengths and challenges that are central to the makeup of each individual administrator. From time to time, assistant principals are promoted to principalships or they may be transferred to another site because of their particular capabilities and the needs of another school. The practical principal must be aware that the system itself may have a need to transfer an assistant principal to another site due to other considerations. These factors include a reassignment from a principalship to an assistant principalship, a temporary reassignment pending a more permanent assignment, or a reassignment for the purpose of training with a high-performing principal.

Regardless of the nature of the reason an assistant principal is either placed or selected to serve under a principal, the practical principal must maximize that delicate blend of talents and abilities of the administrative team to meet the needs of their learning community. This being true, no matter who is chosen to serve with the principal, the practical principal must be responsive to administrative change and be prepared to effectively deal with the impact of those changes on all the stakeholders within the school. The development task of the practical principal in these cases is to minimize any negative impact of the change. The task will include finding a way to maximize the strengths and abilities of the new administrative team.

In my second school assignment as a principal (Werner, again), the school to which I was assigned had an assistant principal who had been in service at that school for several years. When the school's previous principal was promoted to a district directorship, the assistant principal naturally assumed she would be assigned to be the school's next principal. Aware of her principal's impending departure, the assistant principal acted upon her assumption and began proactively organizing the school and the instructional team in preparation for the upcoming school year. She reassigned several teachers to different rate levels and selected different grade chairpersons. This educational leader also made budgetary decisions and plans for purchases for the upcoming school year with her strategic plan for the school.

Unbeknownst to her, the superintendent had decided to transfer me to the school to be the new principal. One can imagine how sticky the situation could be. The practical principal must be ready for all eventualities and this one promised to be particularly difficult. After being told about my new assignment, I made an appointment to see the assistant principal and discuss how we could together help the school continue its progress. It's not hard to imagine the disappointment the assistant principal must have felt in not being selected as the principal. Nonetheless, I believed we had to get through this disappointment, and looked forward to how we could create the best administrative team possible. I had to use my best diplomacy and sensitivity skills to help the assistant principal deal with her disappointment while establishing an effective working relationship that would benefit the school. Although this assistant principal was friendly and collegial, she could never get beyond her disappointment and lack of confidence in the superintendent's decision.

Within weeks, she informed me that she was going to retire at midyear. In addition, she noted that she would be taking considerable time off before her retirement to prepare for some consulting work she planned to undertake. As a result, in my first year at a new assignment, I served without an assistant principal for approximately three-fourths of the school year. The practical principal must be prepared to assume sole responsibility and authority for all aspects of the school operation without warning. The practical principal must also be capable of minimizing the negative aspects of an unhappy or ineffective assistant principal when that situation arises.

During those times, the practical principal must be ever more visible, actively engaged in the day-to-day business of the school, and redouble the investment in building and maintaining an effective learning community within the school. The following school year, I was assigned another assistant principal, who was transferred to me from a post at a school where she was not selected to replace the former principal upon the administrator's retirement. Although the situation could have been much like the first, using sensitivity and openness, we agreed to seize the opportunity to work closely together to help the school improve its performance, knowing that success would later be beneficial to us both.

As a result of our combined efforts and the great work of all the stakeholders within the school, by year's end the school received its first high-performing designation from the state. During that year, utilizing the mentor/mentee relationship, we learned from and supported each other's efforts quite effectively. At the end of that year, the assistant principal was transferred to another school due to the financial constraints facing the district and I served without an assistant principal for the entire next school year.

When the economy experiences a downturn and finances are in jeopardy, the practical principal must be able to embrace challenges and continue to charge toward school excellence despite any perceived barriers to success. The following school year, I once again started the school year without an assistant principal and continued my solo leadership role until late in January, when I received another transfer of a person who had previously served as a principal and was now temporarily assigned to become my new assistant principal. This particular educator only served with me for approximately a month. Although I received some help with routine day-to-day management functions, we both knew the placement was temporary.

In such cases, the practical principal again will minimize any negative impact of temporary personnel assigned to the school. Two months later, another principal was reassigned as assistant principal to my school for the remainder of the year. In a similar vein, we both knew this was a short assignment so the administrative support I received from that administrator was minimal, at best. Regardless of the ebb and flow of administrative assignments, the school was able to maintain its focus throughout the temporary service of both assistant principals and was not negatively affected. As a matter of fact, at the end of this school year, my school received its second high-performing designation from the state in three years.

During my last year of service at that school, I was allowed to select a new assistant principal who had no previous administrative experience. This assistant principal was a go-getter, a team player, a previous teacher well-versed in curriculum, and a person with extraordinary human relations skills. The combination of this pairing as an administrative team created an infectious positive spirit among the staff at school. Virtually every aspect of the school and its programs experienced some form of improvement as a direct result of the effective synthesis of our talents and abilities to harness the best efforts of every stakeholder within the school. Despite a challenging student population and the ever-changing state and federal guidelines for education, we were successful in achieving the highest level of student performance and school recognition in the school's history. Today's principal must embrace every change as an opportunity to learn, grow, and improve. Rather than reel with disappointment or cave in to frustration, the practical principal must increase efforts in the face of these difficulties to provide the kind of leadership and focus the school needs to accomplish its goals and objectives. There's no room for sissies in the principal business. Opportunity, however, is always knocking at the practical principal's door even in the face of adversity.

Before we close this chapter, I (Deana) wanted to mention a few words about the roles of both the assistant and practical principal from a school counselor's perspective. First, when the two are working in tandem, the pairing can be awe-inspiring for all of the employees on the school campus. When an assistant's superior, however, fails to relinquish enough power or responsibility to the second in command, the staff will stop relying on the assistant and go straight to the top. The principal runs the risk of getting bogged down with every small detail of the inner workings of the school, some of which could and should have been delegated to the assistant.

As a counselor (still Deana), I have worked with eight different assistant principals over the course of sixteen years. During my tenure, I have come to not only appreciate the role of the second in command, but have become very close to several of the mostly novice administrators. Their responsibilities have varied a great deal and have run the gamut from the mundane to the unusual and unexpected. Recently, a new assistant principal, looking quite harried, commented to me that he never, with all his years of education, would have thought that he would have to deal with issues such as a student's encopresis. For those of you to whom that may be a new term, it refers to soiling one's self.

I am quite sure such issues were not covered in the educational leadership courses that he took in graduate school. The practical principal, however, has come to expect the unexpected and knows it is all in a day's work, especially at the elementary level. The assistant principal's role in the school's disciplinary measures makes a tremendous impact on the school climate. Ever the effective strategist, the experienced principal can parlay the strengths of the assistant principal and counseling program to reinforce safety, behavior and classroom management skills, and restorative justice in the school.

The second in command, yes, should be able to lead the school in the absence of the principal, but must also be empowered to demonstrate those skills along with and in the presence of the principal. The practical principal can steer the assistant principal toward making sound decisions that improve the quality of the education the students receive. The efficient principal allows room for growth and new ideas, yet knows when to squelch activities that undermine the healthy functioning of the school.

In conclusion, effective assistant principals must possess a wide variety of skills if they are to be useful in helping a school and its principal meet and exceed its goals and objectives. Assistant principals must be self-directed, and must align their decisions and their reasoning with the commonly held philosophy and vision of the principal and the school. The second in command must be an integral part of the school's instructional team, and be capable of addressing and meeting an immediate need without direction from the principal. A good assistant principal must develop and exhibit a capacity to enlist the best and most cooperative efforts of all employees within a learning community. In a best-case scenario, an effective administrative team can actually mirror a great marriage wherein both team members' abilities are complementary.

In a great pairing, a practical principal will serve as a mentor and trainer of the assistant principal. As the assistant principal exhibits the skills and abilities necessary to run the school, the practical principal will strategically delegate additional responsibilities and assignments to the assistant principal. When delegating such responsibilities, the practical principal will establish a process whereby progress and results can be monitored and appropriate feedback given. Ultimately, if the assistant principal is to become a high-performing principal, the principal is responsible for training and being as responsive to the needs of the assistant principals as possible.

In the final analysis, an effective assistant principal can be one of the greatest assets available to a learning community and the principal. No role in the school other than that of principal has such far-reaching impact (Deana would argue here that the counselor's role is on the same level) on the potential success and effective operation of the school than that of the assistant principal.

Chapter Six

Students:
Little Johnny Peed on the Playground

Picture this scenario: one day you're walking about on school grounds, the school day has been underway about an hour, all the students are in the classrooms, and there's no one traveling about the grounds or on the sidewalks. As you do so, you encounter an unusual scene involving one male student, rather conspicuously located on a three-foot wall bordering an amphitheater, apparently imitating a common sculpture of a child that also has a unique fountain function. I'm beginning to think you have a mental image of what I am describing.

During my tenure as principal, this scenario actually took place with an eight-year-old child. The boy was totally unaware that anyone was in the vicinity as he was totally immersed in the creative aspects of his call to nature. As I approached the young man I could not resist the opportunity to say loudly, "Hey, what do you think you're doing?" You can imagine his surprise as he realized the picture he was presenting with his business well in hand, exposed for all to see. Of course, the question was rhetorical, and didn't require an answer. He obviously picked the wrong place at the wrong time to relieve himself and had no acceptable explanation to excuse his behavior.

At some point in an administrator's career, one can be certain he or she will have to deal with an inappropriate elimination issue. The practical principal must be able to deal with undesirable behavior while implementing a consequence to effectively extinguish that behavior with the hope of eliciting a better choice from the student in the future. One thing is certain about being administrator: just when you think you've seen it all, a unique situation will regularly present itself and require immediate attention. In your first years as an administrator, each day will hold a new treasure to be addressed. Over time and with luck and insight, you will be able to say, "Although I am surprised by what a child or student has done, I know I haven't seen it all!" Art Linkletter, a noted talk show host of television's "golden years" coined the phrase, "kids say the darnedest things." In my estimation, kids say and do "the darnedest things." One often assumes all actions of students or children are based upon conscious choice.

Depending on the age of the child, their upbringing, their moral and character development, their impulsivity or reactions in the moment, and a vast array of other factors, this statement may or may not ring true to varying degrees. Many times a student's behavior in the moment is simply a reaction or impulse to an intrusion into their egocentric world from outside sources. Students' behaviors present a challenge and often evoke reactions from the adults who work with them that range from outright hilarity to deep sadness or disappointment. A practical principal must be capable of meeting these behavioral intrusions whether humorous or sad with an effective and appropriate response after weighing every element of the situation, including the context of the event, the individual development of the student, and the impact this event has on everyone affected by it.

The new principal must be well prepared to deal with the full gamut of student behaviors within the context of an educational institution that has ever-increasing demands for academic achievement. Central to this notion is the understanding that connecting with every child in a positive way will make it possible for every child to benefit from the free and appropriate education they deserve to receive. The reactions of the teacher and subsequent disciplinary actions carried out by an administrator for even minor offenses have the potential to undermine the student's educational path very early on. Beginning in kindergarten, a lack of understanding of the underlying causes of a child's behavior can set in motion an unhealthy chain of events for a child resulting in poor school attendance, school phobia, psychosomatic symptoms relating to school, lowered self-confidence with regard to academic achievement, and poor self-esteem.

My own (Deana's) only child experienced a kindergarten hell in which he "retired" the teacher the following year. Gifted and extremely talented musically, he was bored with the regular kindergarten curriculum. Already reading what the teacher deemed as inappropriate material for a boy his age, my son was leaps and bounds ahead of some of his classmates. In addition, he had difficulty understanding why he was not the center of his teacher's universe; after all, one of the perks of being an only child meant that he had his mother's undivided attention. Every single day of his first year in public education appeared to be marred by some type of punitive action taken toward him by the school.

While I recognize that minor infractions can cause major problems in the classroom, more effective measures to deal with such a bright and inattentive student might have yielded a far better outcome. Such measures could have included additional work, time in other classrooms with higher reading levels, peer tutoring, and extra responsibilities to keep him busy. I withdrew my son following that horrendous year and went with him to his next elementary school. While his classroom problems were far from over, they became an exception, rather than the routine. Now, in high school, he is one of the top in his class who still looks back at kindergarten memories that he would like to erase. Despite such a negative experience, he was able to develop strong connections to school that have helped him excel academically and socially.

Within the past decade, highlighted by such events as Columbine and the myriad acts of violence against employees and students in many of our schools throughout the nation, a lack of school connectedness and sense of belonging have complicated the role of the practical principal in providing educational opportunities to all children within a safe and nurturing environment. A mere fifty years ago the top offenses students were referred to the office for disciplinary assistance included chewing gum and excessive talking in class.

Today, assault and battery, possession and use of drugs and alcohol, defiant behaviors, and property destruction comprise the bulk of disciplinary referrals that principals must address. Although most forward-thinking and enlightened educators agree that every child can and will learn, the common thread to the quality and effectiveness of this learning is linked to the quality of the connectedness students feel to the educational institutions they attend. Proof that children learn from their educational environment can be seen in the recent event highlighted by the media, where several eight- and nine-year-old students identified with special needs embraced and utilized "cooperative learning strategies" to plan and implement a violent assault upon their exceptional education teacher.

In the true case being referred to, the children used all the essential elements of cooperative learning wherein a leader was elected, appropriate group roles were designated (up to and including individual assignments for the collection and delivery to the school of supplies needed to carry out the act), and an actual plan to complete the act was detailed and discussed by all participants. Had it not been for a student reporting the plan shared by one of the group members, a teacher may have been lethally injured by her students. The apparent motivation for this plan was the perceived unfairness of the teacher. The practical principal must understand the underlying motivations for inappropriate behavior to be successful in shaping more positive behavior in students as they grow and learn within their school.

To illustrate this point, I (Werner) would like to share a situation in which a student's behavior, taken at face value, may have resulted in serious long-term ramifications for the student had it not been dealt with appropriately. Many times a student's behavior is viewed only from a behavioral standpoint without consideration of its context and other salient information that may actually reinforce inappropriate behavior. The practical principal is very aware that behavior does not occur in a vacuum. One case in point involves an eleven-year-old exceptional-education male student who was rather large for his age and often appeared to make the wrong choices when it came to his peers and teachers. Although we had a great rapport as principal and student, he was what I call a "frequent flyer" when it came to referrals to the office.

This student had numerous verbal and physical conflicts with peers and adults whom he perceived as picking on him and being unfair when they had to deal with his behavioral issues. He had all the indicators of someone who was slowly becoming disconnected from the institution that was trying to help him. One day this young man came to school appearing more easily agitated by adults and children on the walkway. When asked to go to his classroom, he was openly defiant toward adults. Although this student had never really been a bully and usually wasn't physically aggressive toward others, on this day he was walking around campus pushing kids out of his way, muttering insults, and generally being mean to others. It almost appeared as if he wanted to get sent home or be suspended. Generally, our staff members went out of their way to avoid confronting a student who seemed out of sorts while trying to assist the individual in finding better ways to get along with others. Our goal was and always has been to keep a child in school learning and, hopefully, happy every day.

The exceptional student, however, was not receptive to our assistance on this date. In my discussion with him, he actually said, "just take me home; I'm in a bad mood and I'm going to hurt somebody if you don't take me home." Not wanting to give up on him, I took him to the office to get him off the walkway and give him some time out. He only became increasingly agitated and defiant, and even aggressive toward me. Finally, I just came out and said, "This isn't like you. You look like you just want to get into trouble today." Suddenly his whole countenance changed and he became tearful. Then, he blurted out, "There's something wrong with my mom and I just have to go home."

Many times, children with special needs, or just children in general, do not know how to understand and express their own feelings. A practical principal must be able to seize those moments to get at the root of the problem rather than simply reacting to their behavior as the voice of authority. In the ensuing conversation, I discovered that the student's mother and her boyfriend had a violent argument immediately prior to the boy and his sister leaving for school. As the argument ensued and became more physical, the mother told her children to go on to school. Above his protests, the boy and his sisters were forced out the door and sent to school, while the mother and the boyfriend continued their violent interaction.

Not having the ability to adequately articulate his concern about his mother upon arrival at the school, all he knew was that he was afraid for his mother's safety. He immediately acted upon the only way that he knew might result in getting him returned home by creating a problem for children and teachers. After all, he believed in his heart if he acted really mean to people or appeared to want to hurt somebody, surely someone would take him home. I did, in fact, take the student home that day and when we arrived, the front door to the home was wide open, the couch and the living room furniture were overturned, and broken debris was strewn about the house. I asked him to remain outside while I went inside, for I was prepared to find an injured mother in need of assistance. Completing my search, I found no one in the home. Somewhat relieved but still concerned, I tried to talk him into going back to school with me.

As we were having this conversation, his mother emerged from a neighbor's house. Her visible injuries included a black eye and cut lip. She explained that she had sent her children to school to keep them safe from her boyfriend's rage. This young man truly loved his mother and out of a sense of protection sacrificed himself to have an excuse to go home and make sure she was safe. To this day, this event still has a profoundly emotional impact upon me. It was on that day that I suddenly realized in my development as a budding principal that the practical principal must strive to understand the motivations of behavior, whether conscious or unconscious to the student if he is going to be of effective assistance to the child experiencing behavioral distress.

An understanding principal must accept the reality that some of his students live in a subculture of violence where physical, psychological, and emotional abuse occurs frequently and at random. Realistically, the best place the child may be in a given day is quite possibly the classroom. The school may well be the source of the best food available to many children and the cleanest and most pleasant environment they have available to them on a daily basis. Additionally, it also may be by far the safest place where they receive the best attention and nurturing each day. This frame of reference should temper and guide the reactions and responses of the practical principal to the unacceptable behavioral presentations exhibited by students. The practical principal must develop an understanding of the demographic makeup of the school, the economic opportunities available to the community in which it is located, and the various other factors that impact a child's growth and development away from the school setting. These are all essential insights for the practical principal to possess to positively shape the learning community toward the accomplishment of commonly shared goals.

Although bigotry and ignorance may be taught and supported in some homes, we are convinced that children are born into this world basically accepting of one another and imbued with certain humane qualities. Children want acceptance for themselves and others. They look to adults for guidance, nurturance, and support. They are inherently trusting by nature, but learn to mistrust through their daily interactions with the environment and other people with whom they have contact. In support of these assertions, I am reminded of the scene that still warms my heart to this day of two kindergarten children walking down the sidewalk, coming to the office to deliver their teacher's daily attendance roster. Typically, teachers at the elementary level send children to the office in pairs to make sure they get there safely and in the appropriate amount of time.

As I observed these children who were unaware of my presence, I was reassured about the goodness in human nature, as a black male and a white female walked together hand-in-hand conversing happily and acceptingly as they proceeded to accomplish their assigned task. From the earliest days, it is clear that a single school culture that seeks to connect all stakeholders to a sense of belonging within the institution can be an effective agent of positive change and inclusion for all members of our society now and into the future.

Chapter Seven

Parents: The Buck Stops Here

As a practical principal, you have accepted a position wherein one-third of your leadership team may or may not be fully committed and invested in what you are doing. Although parents can help you present a united front toward achieving a brighter future for children, they may all have different perspectives on how to reach that goal. Prepare to have your eyes opened to the wide range of "support" you will receive from parents in an effort to improve "student performance" while providing exemplary educational opportunities for every student within your school. It is a guarantee that on a daily basis you as the principal will spend a substantial portion of your time informally or formally interacting with parents as you go about your duties. These interactions with parents will span conversations ranging from those in which the parent is righteously indignant (i.e., outright "ticked off") to those where the parent is totally cooperative and supportive (productive home/school partnerships).

As a practical principal, you will have to deal with allegations of "inadequate supervision," alleged insults, intimidations, bullying, and injuries of students, disagreements regarding grading, classroom assignments, grade-level teacher assignment, and apparent parental bigotry, insensitivity, and intolerance regarding students or staff members at your school. As an administrator, you will experience every level of parent involvement from absolutely no support or input to total immersion in school improvement and school-based decision making by parent stakeholders. Yes, my friend, you are now the principal and every parent at one time or another will demand answers from you to the magical question, how could you let "(you fill in the blank)" happen to my child at your school?

On many occasions, you may be totally unaware of the issue until a concerned parent arrives at the school "loaded for bear." These situations are often likely to occur right before school is released at the end of the day and involve a car pulling up in the school parking lot in a rather hurried fashion and screeching to a halt. The parent will hastily leave the car, steaming toward your front door, obviously agitated. No matter how small the issue, its weight may be magnified by the parent's concern for the child's well-being and rights. Whatever happens after the initial confrontation with the parent depends upon the practical principal's skill in defusing the anger and reassuring the parent that the matter will be addressed quickly and fairly.

The principal can turn a bad situation into a productive and unifying moment by expressing genuine concern without obvious threats of retaliation toward the parent. A relentless and repetitive focus upon expressing a desire to help, using a diplomatic approach (even when you feel fear and panic inside), will make it much easier to defuse the situation. This type of approach will create better conditions under which the principal can effectively assist the parent in addressing concerns regarding the students. Even the most difficult parents, in the most agitated state, when presented with the right attitude and reassurance by the principal wants to allow the school to solve a problem for them. Often, parental relationships starting off on rocky ground evolve to become strong, home–school partnerships when the principal handles these initial confrontations with calm, respectful, and professional resolve.

Keep in mind, we are not condoning or supporting inappropriate, threatening behavior from parents, nor do we expect one to accept it. We are simply saying the most effective leader must weigh all options and deal with each event or situation in context and with an eye toward the potential interactions and relationship you want to maintain with the parent in the future. A parent who is verbally abusive to a staff member should be redirected in the most tactful way possible. Students and teachers alike have the right not to be harassed. Giving voice to hostile parents (or abusive staff members for that matter) empowers them to continue to bully, threaten, and sabotage the educational process. Allowing such rage to swell without being addressed swiftly leaves staff members open to becoming the unwitting target of potential violence.

There are times when a principal has to deal with a parent to provide appropriate placement and strategic support for their child when the parent may be cognitively functioning at a very low level. Some parents may have diagnosed learning disabilities or face other challenges that may interfere with their ability to fully understand the educational process and their child's rights. Cases such as these do not diminish the importance of providing respect that all parents deserve along with information that may be easily understood. A practical principal must have the ability to relate in an appropriate fashion to all parents regardless of their level of education, economic challenge, or cognitive ability to enhance their cooperative efforts as they strive together to provide optimum developmental experiences and learning opportunities for their children. A school leader must always strive to develop strong productive partnerships with all parents in spite of challenges that may threaten to compromise those partnerships.

Sometimes timing and a conspiracy of coincidence may work together to lead parents to come to an incorrect conclusion regarding the school or its teachers. A simple worksheet can even become a catalyst for parental meltdown and potential complaint to the principal or district person. One day a child who was working with a speech and language therapist on the correct articulation of the letter "K" in beginning, middle, and ending presentations of words was given a worksheet to take home with which to guide his assigned articulation practice. Since the work was given during the week in which we celebrated Dr. Martin Luther King Jr.'s birthday, the worksheet had a portrait of Dr. King taking up the majority of the page with three large letter Ks across the bottom third of the page. The therapist's instructions were to "take the worksheet home and practice sounding out the letter 'K' with your parents at home." The students were advised to ask parents to help them find things in the home that have the letter "K" in their names and practice saying them to their parents. When they finished their practice, they were asked to color the picture of Dr. King and the letter K and place it in the speech notebook to use later.

Later that day, the speech student misplaced the paper. Prior to student dismissal, another student found the worksheet on the floor, placed it his backpack and took it home. Upon finding the work that evening, the parent concluded that one of the child's teachers at school must be a racist. Upon seeing the picture of Dr. Martin Luther King Jr., accompanied by the "three large "Ks," he was certain that some teacher at the school was extolling the virtues of the Ku Klux Klan. Of course, the following morning, the father of the black child demanded an immediate investigation into which one of the principal's teachers was promulgating and reinforcing racism in her teachings. After about an hour-long meeting the principal reassured the parent she would investigate the matter and get back with him. She ultimately had to talk to the classroom teacher, the boy who was the speech student, and a speech therapist to get to the bottom of the issue. This principal spent approximately two hours dealing with the perceived problem that turned out to be just a harmless coincidence, an activity that was not well thought out, but with no malice intended.

A practical principal knows that even in the face of an obvious misunderstanding, it is best to take the time to investigate the claims and concerns to provide appropriate support, understanding, and resolution of a parent's issue. A less concerned or involved principal who does not possess such skill and understanding will ultimately hear about the problem again, most likely from a higher authority in the district or potentially from the media sensationalizing the issue and demanding immediate attention. Again, giving parents an opportunity to be heard while reassuring them of a desire to help and seek a resolution to the issue that is fair, appropriate, and correct will cement the cooperative partnership between parents who are expressing the concern and the principal who seeks to address it not only in the moment, but for future interactions as well.

Interactions with parents can often be humorous, also requiring the practical principal to think on his feet or choose to sit down. On one occasion, a parent who had recently been released from prison after serving a lengthy sentence for assault and battery arrived in my office angrily shouting every obscenity under the sun at me. Lucky for me, I (Werner) had spent four years in the U.S. Navy and was very conversant in the vernacular he chose to use. Although I had no intention of using the same language, I completely comprehended the meaning imbedded in his words. This stocky man actually had a Mohawk hairstyle and multiple large tattoos visible on every inch of his skin. This gentleman's complaint was, "I'm tired of these kids living in the neighborhood around this school picking on my boy." He said, "My boy tells me he has reported it to you on several occasions and you didn't do anything about it. I'm here to get this settled now once and for all." The practical principal must be diplomatic and reassuring even in times of stress, while trying to never let the parent "see them sweat."

All of this information was delivered to me immediately in one continuous tirade, interspersed with profanity, as he walked into my office. I stood up to greet him and as I did, he walked right up in my personal space and threatened to "kick my scrawny, baldheaded, posterior (he used another word for posterior)." I suddenly realized he was so agitated and out of control that I believed he would hit me. I immediately sat down. In my head, I reasoned that most people would not hit somebody sitting down with glasses on, and, if they did, I would have less distance to travel in falling to the floor and thus I would minimize my chances for additional collateral injury from the potential attack. It's funny what goes through one's mind in contemplating strategies for dealing with threatening situations. My choice to sit down actually caused him to stop his tirade.

In a puzzled way he looked at me and then proceeded to sit down himself. From that point forward, I was able to genuinely express my concern for his issue and my intent to help him obtain a suitable and fair remedy to his problem. Following about a forty-five-minute discussion, he stood up when I rose so that we could shake hands. He believed that I would handle the matter fairly and would advise him of the outcome as quickly as I could. His children attended my school for approximately three more years after the incident. Whenever this particular parent had an issue to discuss, we were able to deal with it effectively and to his satisfaction from that time forward. Even under duress, the practical principal must strive to build productive working relationships with every parent on behalf of children, whose best interest they share.

A principal will have interactions with parents who are angry, parents who desire a remedy to a problem, parents who seem to want to micromanage every aspect of their child's instruction, parents who are operating on faulty assumptions or incorrect information, and parents who believe the school has failed their children in some way, shape, or form. As a principal, I have had knives pulled on me, have been verbally and physically threatened, have been called upon for comfort and advice, and have been told by parents that I was the next best thing to peanut butter.

I have had parents, usually within the first two sentences of their shouting at me, threaten to "lawyer up" and have me fired or sued. What is odd to me is that so many people on limited income typically imply that they have lawyers on retainer when I as a principal do not have one on retainer myself. Nonetheless, in twenty-nine years in education, I've not been sued by a parent or had to face a judge for my decisions as an educator or school principal. On numerous occasions, parents have complained to the district office or the superintendent before giving me a chance to help them with their problem. Over the years, despite parental claims or complaints, using the approach to parent assistance discussed above, I have not been instructed to change my decisions or had them overridden as a result of district intervention.

The non-threatening principal knows there will always be someone who disagrees with his decisions. He also knows that complaints and misunderstandings will be something he should always expect to deal with in the daily performance of his leadership functions. The practical principal must necessarily understand that in adhering to appropriate process, policy, and procedure, his decisions will prevail under district or legal scrutiny. Principals focusing upon building positive interactive capacity and parental relationships within their schools will create and maintain those assurances that will guarantee parents the appropriate concern, attention, and resolution of any issue they have with the school or its staff. Yes, parents can be a source of challenge or of strong, ongoing support for the school and its principal. It is ultimately up to the strong principal to mold these relationships to become mutually rewarding and productive for all parties involved.

Chapter Eight

Testing 1, 2, 3: Are We Measuring Up?

Some would argue that the process of standardized testing and student assessment has become the bane of a school faculty's existence. In recent history, education has gone from very little, if any, formalized student assessment and instructional accountability, to an environment that has been characterized by some as "NCLB hell." With the passage of the "No Child Left Behind" (NCLB) federal law, many parents, teachers, and administrators feel that they are doomed by an accountability nightmare in their combined efforts to provide the highest quality of educational opportunities possible for children. Most educators would agree that the goal of public education is to fully tap the combined potentials of parents, children, and administrators to help all children maximize their respective abilities to become self-actualized.

The current environment of assessment and accountability, though, is creating great cause for concern in all educational stakeholders. It is a noble goal to state that no child should be left out or left behind in our "free and appropriate" educational process. Never once in our careers though have we ever heard a teacher utter the words, "I am going to leave that little girl or little boy behind." The mere thought of these words suggests an implied insult to the integrity of teachers as they strive to make a difference in the lives of their students. We have yet to meet a teacher who seriously wants a child to fail at learning or self-actualization. To the contrary, throughout our combined careers spanning a total of over forty years, we have both found teachers to be among some of the most caring, conscientious, and idealistic human beings with whom we have had the privilege to interact, work, and share a sense of community and purpose.

Beneficial student testing and other assessments are useful tools in evaluating the effectiveness and quality of educational strategies with children. As educators, we are supposed to use effective assessment instruments to measure whether our instructional efforts and content meet program objectives and goals. Assessments should assist educators in aligning teaching materials with expected instructional outcomes. Appropriate measures can help us guide and develop our instruction to meet the individual and aggregate developmental needs of our students.

Assessments can be diagnostic and prescriptive for individual students, or can be used to compare one aggregate population to a standard or a norm group. A variety of tests are available to assist the educator in understanding student performance. In many states, the Dynamic Indicators of Basic Early Literacy Skills (DIBELS) are administered three times a year to students in kindergarten through sixth grade. Such tests are designed to help teachers assess literacy development, fluency, and reading skills. These types of standardized tests also include progress monitoring between the official testing windows. Other standardized testing differs across the states, but often includes some type of norm-referenced test that assesses reading and other subject areas as the students get older. The standardized tests are supposed to be aligned to the curriculum or course of study by grade level. Data from these tests were once used to help identify strengths and weaknesses in student performance and instructional methodology. The stakes, however, are much higher now than ever before, even for students. Across the country, many high school students, despite having earned the required Carnegie units, must also pass some type of graduation exam to graduate.

Within the past two decades, political issues and fiscal accountability have demanded that assessments be used to attest to the quality of the school's instructional programs and its teachers. Rather than being used as a measure for instructional alignment, testing has become the goal-focused result of education. Assessments are now typically used as accountability tools to justify or diminish school funding. They have become means whereby national and state departments of education monitor the apparent efficacy or ineffectiveness of schools. Testing results now purportedly determine whether or not schools are implementing the required and mandated instructional programs effectively. In effect, assessment as a natural and important technique integral in improving educational success has now become an accountability tool at cross purposes with its original intent.

A byproduct of the NCLB legislation has been the grading of schools to supposedly help the general public understand the quality of their return for their public education dollar. Elaborate schemes have been developed by each state throughout our nation to enable the grading of the school on a scale comparable to that of a student's report card. To ensure that "no child is left behind," these grading systems examine student performance across all demographic areas and within demographic classifications so that no child is left out in the instructional process. The grading process supposedly helps to assure that regardless of subgroup membership such as race, sex, handicap condition, level of income, type of family structure, language, or nationality, every child is provided the proper and appropriate educational growth opportunity within the school.

NCLB grading systems and definitions are important, yet not widely understood. I (Deana) once received a call from a parent who was desperate to see her son graduate. The mother asked about that law that would make sure that her child was not left behind. While I could appreciate her genuine concern, the misperception about NCLB legislation is widespread. An entire chapter is dedicated to some of the legalese that educators must deal with. By national guidelines, schools must meet "adequate progress" in every demographic subgroup to be considered an effective and properly performing school. The term "adequate progress" does not mean simply adequate progress, however; it means perfect progress. For adequate progress to be realized by a school, 100 percent of the indicators of "adequate progress" across every demographic category expressed within the school's population must be achieved. Recently, it was suggested that no more than 30 percent of our nation's schools had achieved adequate progress as measured by their annual assessments.

These annual assessments are not standardized across the United States and have considerable variance from one state to another. Where one state may have an extraordinarily restrictive assessment process and criteria for school grading and adequate progress determination, another state may have much "softer" assessment processes and grading criteria. Thus, comparing one state to another using this notion is much like comparing apples to oranges. Nonetheless, the unceasing intrusion of national and state accountability criteria upon local schools has created an atmosphere of extreme stress and fear among educators. Schools unable to achieve adequate progress within a five-year period are required to be "restructured," externally monitored, and governed by others. Public schools can be closed down and reconstituted as charter schools while new faculties and staff members are hired to replace teachers and administrators who are released and asked to transfer.

In college, the goals of assessment and testing appeared very clear. Effective assessment could be used to diagnose and prescribe instructional strategies and techniques to better meet the instructional needs of the student population. Standardized assessments were used to help teachers and administrators understand individual and group growth in their content knowledge and in their learned skill application within their schools. Assessments also helped identify staff-development needs to enhance instructional and student learning throughout the school. With these convictions as fundamental assumptions regarding the appropriate use of instructional assessment, the practical principal can use the data derived from various measures to determine which students might benefit from additional intervention.

Those particular students were ones whose performance indicated less than adequate learning and skill mastery so that the teacher may focus individual efforts upon overcoming these performance shortfalls. The practical principal can use student performance data from a collection of assessment instruments to understand how to alter individual instructional efforts and strategies to meet individual student performance deficits. In turn, principals can use group or classroom performance data to identify areas of teacher strength or challenge when it comes to the instruction of subject area content as well.

As a byproduct of the NCLB process, a national trend is emerging to use assessment data to drive improved student performance on required accountability assessments to higher levels through the provision of "pay for performance" and financial school incentive programs. This trend seems to take its focus from the view that student performance can be improved by providing teachers and schools bonuses for gains evidenced on adopted standardized assessments required by the state. In many cases, however, the assessment instruments used to measure these gains or growth across content areas may not be comparable, and therefore may reward some with less rigorous instructional content and softer assessments at the expense of those with a more demanding content and more difficult assessments.

National research regarding pay-for-performance programs and school recognition incentives vary greatly in their findings concerning the utility of this approach in impacting student learning and enhancing instructional efficacy from one school or system to another. Generally speaking, teacher unions, both nationally and locally, disagree with this approach to employee compensation or the philosophy upon which it is based. Such an approach generally pits one teacher against another, creates divisiveness and dissension among school staffs, creates mistrust and apprehension between school administrators and their staff members, and has yet to demonstrate a cause-and-effect relationship between actual enhanced student learning and improved instructional efficacy among teachers.

Currently, throughout our nation, a broad consensus believes that the NCLB initiative has not achieved its original desired intent. Two years ago, the then national secretary of education stated in a press conference, "the No Child Left Behind initiative is comparable to that of a child in the developmental stage of the terrible twos." She might have meant was that although this concept is in its infancy and has some serious issues to be dealt with, it is something that must be endured and is just part of the growth process. At that time, no indication was given of any intent to produce some uniformity among the accountability assessment processes across the fifty states within our nation, and no indication of any desire to create an accountability system that truly compares apples to apples.

It is clear that teacher turnover throughout the United States is rampant. Most experts agree that well over 50 percent of the teachers who were in service five years ago are no longer in the profession today. NCLB standards require teachers to be "highly qualified" in the content area or grade level they are assigned to teach. Schools that are eligible to receive and accept federal funding to support their educational programs are required to ensure that all their instructional personnel are "highly qualified" for their instructional assignments within their schools. Failure to maintain this commitment may result in a loss of funding for schools that otherwise depend on this funding to provide a continuum of services that have been deemed necessary to students. Equally discouraging, a nationwide push exists (due to the national teacher shortage) to encourage and support alternative teacher certification programs for degree personnel outside of education to become teachers.

I (Deana) actually have an alternative certification. I was (and still am) a licensed professional counselor when I entered the school system with no experience in the public schools other than in a counseling role. I now teach at the college level and have been in the public schools for over fifteen years. During both our tenures, we have witnessed dramatic changes and shifts among teachers. This year, in the district for which I (Werner) work, 50 percent of the teachers hired were seeking alternative certification because they were not professionally trained educators. At the end of the school year, one-fourth of the 50 percent who were seeking alternative certification were not recommended back for employment or decided to leave the profession on their own.

Should this trend continue; the future for education as an institution looks bleak and challenging at best, especially when coupled with unrealistic levels of accountability for student performance and educational effectiveness. Regardless of state and national proclivity toward testing and school grading, the practical principal must focus upon how to lead teachers to meet and exceed difficulties and challenges they face in the future. The practical principal, guided by the ideals of effective measurement techniques, can still hope to provide effective instructional leadership and development to the learning community while seeking to connect all staff members to each other and the higher ideals they seek to achieve together. As the educational pendulum swings from one extreme to the other, the single unifying influence in maintaining an effective and cohesive learning community over time is now and will always be the practical principal.

Chapter Nine

Law: Crossing the Legal Line

Historically, school administrators have never faced more legal requirements and potential legal challenges in the performance of their daily duties than they do at this time. From federal requirements and laws such as Public Law 94-142 (the federal law establishing required educational services to handicapped students) and "No Child Left Behind" (NCLB) legislation to state laws and statutes governing public education, to local school district policies and procedures established to implement state and federal laws, today's principal faces potential court challenges to virtually every decision he makes on a daily basis. We currently live in a litigious society that at every turn is encouraged by television and media advertisements to pursue legal action against anyone and everyone who violates, abuses, or ignores the rights of the individual student and his or her family.

For this reason, it is incumbent upon the school principal to be familiar with all state, federal, and local laws and regulations governing and guaranteeing the effective operation and appropriate provision of public education programs within the school to which he or she is assigned. As we stated in an earlier chapter, not only are parents quick to threaten that they will obtain a lawyer to assure their demands are met within our schools, an abundance of advocacy groups and organizations are eager to champion their causes of action. The practical principal must tread very carefully so as not to cross the legal line involving student, parent, and staff rights. Unfortunately, the legal line often seems blurred or obscured by various issues at play.

From testing to harassment, and many policies in between, a practical principal must be well-versed or at least aware of the possible legal ramifications of specific actions. As a rule, administrators and counselors often work very hard to protect parent and student rights by following the letter of the law.

Confidentiality is of primary importance, especially when it involves educational records and testing. The practical principal must be able to recognize when a threat is a threat and a promise is a promise. Likewise, the practical principal must treat a genuine concern by a parent or community member as an issue that must be addressed and resolved without the need for external intervention.

Proactive principals, through experience and a detailed knowledge of the composition of the stakeholders of their learning community, must be acutely aware of serious issues that can become insurmountable and difficult to resolve. The possible negative consequences of not adhering to federal and state laws can result in loss of federal or state funding, restructuring and reconstitution of existing school structures, or at worst, can result in the termination or incarceration of the supervising administrator of the school. One of the quickest ways a principal can lose a job is to be arrested for the deliberate and intentional mismanagement of public school funding or not following the state system's canon of ethical practices. Thus, the practical principal must understand and operate the federal, state, and local laws governing provision of public education programs.

Like the Civil Rights Act of 1964 and Plessy versus Ferguson before it, the NCLB federal legislation changed the course of history. In one piece of legislation, all public education programs within the United States that accepted federal funding were placed under an accountability microscope. This type of scrutiny has virtually changed the curriculums we teach, the goals and objectives of the schools our students attend, and redefined the appropriate outcomes public education as an institution is supposed to achieve. This legislation heightened the public's awareness of the importance of testing and measurement of student performance in all of our schools. It also set into motion an unstoppable chain of events that would ultimately lead to the reconstitution and restructuring of schools that repeatedly failed to meet appropriate student performance standards across all demographic groups within those schools.

The beginnings of the law can be traced back to *Brown v. Board of Education*, wherein the U.S. Supreme Court outlawed racial segregation in public schools fifty years ago. With the idea of ensuring an education that is more inclusive, responsive, and fair, the law dictates certain achievement gains for students in schools, teacher qualifications, and instruction. Should any of the mandates not be met, as in schools not meeting what is commonly referred to as "adequate yearly progress" (AYP) with regard to test scores, reductions in federal funding may ensue. In a worst-case scenario, faculty and staff of the school can be reassigned and replaced by new faculty and staff or the school can be closed completely. It is therefore important that the practical principal understand the goals and the purposes of the school's testing programs, and monitor them completely for accuracy, security, and for consistency of implementation.

When it comes to administering standardized tests set forth by the state department of education, certified personnel could potentially have their licenses or teaching certificates revoked if test security is breached. From the standpoint of giving or proctoring the tests, most educators tend to be over-obsessive about security issues. The wise principal follows protocol when dealing with circumstances that affect the integrity of the testing environment. This becomes especially problematic when a student "hurls his breakfast" on the actual testing document. Incidents like this do actually occur due to test anxiety and other factors, and a specific procedure is in place on how to bag up the test document and handle the situation. Today's teachers feel the pressure to teach the subjects they are required and assess their students' performance appropriately. They know that testing anomalies or irregularities can affect their teaching certificates and their reputations as educators, and their livelihoods may be in jeopardy. Additionally, the pressure to earn a better school grade and show AYP creates a great deal of stress and fear in the teachers who provide the daily instruction and administer the required assessments measuring the mastery of that instructional content of their students.

With the ever-increasing pressure created by high stakes testing, test security violations are not unheard of. Even principals are not immune to trying to increase their scores in a less than scrupulous manner. Unfortunately, I (Deana) was a building test coordinator for a site that had an aide who cheated for a student receiving special services. Upon hearing rumors, I asked for the investigation to be conducted and was appalled at the findings. The aide in this case indicated that he felt that his actions were in the best interest of the students. Others who try to bend the rules, make answer keys, or copy standardized tests may fear their jobs are on the line if test scores do not improve, so they justify their drastic measures. Teachers who are monitoring or proctoring exams may even repeat pneumonic reminders to students attempting to answer test items. This strategy is obviously impermissible, and when observed or reported creates an obligation for the school principal or district personnel to investigate the situation and seek appropriate punitive consequences for the teacher in question.

As misguided as the assistance typically is, the teacher often cites the cognitive functioning of the student and the resulting unfairness of the assessment, or other factors as rationalizations for attempting to breach test security by assisting students on standardized tests. Individuals who are caught violating assessment policies do indeed lose their jobs, and perhaps their sense of identity, because they possibly may not be able to seek another position

with a school system. In a larger sense, when censured for such an abuse such teachers may actually lose their state certification and/or their ability to practice as a teacher ever again. The articulate principal espouses the importance of maintaining adequate test security in test distribution and implementation to all personnel assisting in the assessment process.

Effective principals maintain the integrity of the assessment process from receipt and storage of testing at the school site, to daily assessment during the testing window, to the final organization and packaging of all test materials to be shipped to and scored by the test's publisher. In adhering to these caveats, the principal can ensure an appropriate and secure suitable performance-assessment process for his or her students and school.

Within public education, special education generates more paperwork and requires more documentation than any other area. The Individuals with Disabilities Education Improvement Act of 2004 (IDEA) is the federal law that dictates services for students with disabilities. In following IDEA regulations and other rules, schools must ensure that students with disabilities receive all the services that they are entitled to. Such provisions require a myriad of documentation and a long paper trail to verify the receipt of accommodations, modifications, and other services. One missing document could lead to a courtroom challenge by a child rights' advocate. The tedious paperwork, therefore, serves a very real purpose to make certain the child's rights are not violated and that the teacher, and ultimately the school, has followed the individual educational plan (IEP) for each student.

The school administrator must be attuned to the specific needs of all students on the campus. When services are not being provided, administrators are often called into question. The practical principal must be able to address deficiencies in services without threatened enforcement from a lawyer or other third-party external to the school. The wise school leader must act out of genuine and immediate concern for the child. Of course, the practical principal should always be mindful of what actions or inaction might lead to a lawsuit. Practical principals should possess a working knowledge and understanding of their students' needs and challenges so that they can suggest, implement, and monitor a seamless delivery of appropriate interventions and services to best meet the respective needs of every student within their school. The principal who knows the student body, understands its respective challenges and developmental needs, and orchestrates the appropriate instructional delivery to and for that population will have the best ability to positively influence the growth of student performance with the school they strive to lead toward excellence.

Another area ripe for litigation that presents a potential threat to all principals involves contract implementation. Most school systems have a teacher's association or teacher's union that bargains on behalf of instructional and noninstructional personnel to protect their rights and interests and assure as employees they are treated fairly. These "contracts" enumerate agreed-upon rights and responsibilities of the parties governed by the contract (management and unions). As such, these contracts are legal documents that bind all parties to agreed-upon practices, rights, and responsibilities. They dictate the way in which employers interact with employees and appropriate working-place expectations that are binding upon all parties. As a member of a union, teachers and other personnel pay dues for certain benefits, including legal representation. Teachers' rights are many and varied. The steps that a practical principal takes with regard to disciplinary action, reprimands, and other steps must be carefully planned and supported by school board policy protected by the authority of the superintendent and school board.

The increased amount of public scrutiny on schools has placed pressure on school officials to act quickly when a teacher's actions are called into question. Nonetheless, appropriate investigative procedures, employee due process, and appropriate objectivity in the investigative process must be provided to ensure these actions are appropriately dealt with and handled to their ultimate conclusion. Of course, administrators must act with swift determination to protect students. The well-publicized cases of sexual abuse involving teachers and students underscore the important role of school leaders in providing appropriate student protection. Parents place their trust in school officials to react rapidly and decisively on behalf of their children. In teaching a recent child psychology course to college students, most of whom were education majors, I (Deana) seized upon the opportunity to discuss some of the egregious acts that occur on a campus. My discussions included such topics as sexual abuse, bullying, and other forms of violence against children. One female student reacted quite angrily to the discussions and accused me of presenting "salacious" material just to keep the class interested. In addition, she stated that such information need not be reviewed because the media had already covered it, including the "Oprah show." The same future educator expressed her dismay over a bullying presentation that she found offensive due to the explicit language of the teens in the video that I used. The following week after I led that particular discussion on teen violence and bullying, a high school student took her life due to a cyber-bullying incident.

The media oftentimes tends to sensationalize dramatic events that occur on a campus. The repeated media exposure to such acts may desensitize some to the very real and dangerous issues facing our young people in schools today, or may lead others (like my outspoken college student) to just not want to hear about it anymore. As a society, we cannot oversimplify, ignore, sweep under the carpet, or just choose to look the other way when trying to equip young people with safeguards for their perilous journey to adulthood. A practical principal must be able to make a public statement to media officials regarding an event that may have taken place on the school grounds. At one time or another, every principal will be interviewed by a television or newspaper reporter and put on the spot to disclose details surrounding incidents involving safety or other issues that may have occurred at their school. Because these inquiries often come immediately following an alleged event prior to all the facts being uncovered and the conclusion of an investigation, the school official will have to keep his remarks to a minimum. The educational leader must restate to the reporter their primary concern is the safety and well-being of the school's student population and additional information will be forthcoming when the investigation is complete. In so doing, a practical principal preserves confidentiality, the integrity of the investigative process, and the individual rights of all students and staff members that may have participated in the event.

By the nature of our unique roles as educators we are in many ways surrogate parents, confidantes, and, during the school day, guardians of the safety and well-being of the children entrusted to our care. We know that on any given day students may experience trauma at home, school, or somewhere on the path in between. Nevertheless, we are called upon by our students to help them, nurture them, and cultivate their knowledge along the way as the resilient child develops and blossoms within our rooms and behind our doors. To foster such growth and resilience, the staff must be well supported and well prepared to react to and handle the adversity that may impact the daily lives of our children. Just as every student has the right to attend school without being harassed or bullied, a school employee also has those same rights.

A practical principal will follow the letter of the law in preserving the rights of everyone within the entire learning community including all staff members. Like a benevolent caretaker, the seasoned educator must walk a thin line between what is right and wrong, while ensuring that all individuals have the ability and appropriate facilitative conditions within which to grow and flourish while attempting to realize their utmost potential. Along with the difficulty and potential liability inherent in federal, state, and local laws, so too comes the comfort and assurance that these noble pieces of legislation offer to all of the stakeholders within our schools. A practical principal must often act as a pseudo-guardian ad litem while sometimes functioning as the sheriff, judge, and jury, as well as chief watchdog protecting and guaranteeing the rights of every participant with a vested interest in the outcomes in the schoolhouse. A practical principal will take care in obeying the law to not cross the legal line.

Chapter Ten

Technology: Look What We Can Do!

An educator who has worked in the field for any length of time can attest to the fact that available instructional resources have evolved exponentially with the rapid technological advances in our society. In 1979, the state-of-the-art technology in rural school districts, particularly with regard to the production of daily student work (commonly referred to as "worksheets"), was the movement from manual, hand-cranked mimeograph machines to electric, self-inking mimeograph machines. In retrospect, this low-tech innovation may seem a minor technological innovation. What it did allow, however, was a high-speed, high-volume student work production process, allowing teachers to enhance the drill and practice process of students across subject areas throughout grade levels in the school.

During its time, the mimeograph machine effectively became a school-based printing press that mass produced quantities of support materials for teachers to improve student instruction and performance within their schools. In a mere twenty-nine years, technological advancement within our schools has vastly improved and radically changed instructional methodology as well as student assessment and evaluation processes.

In retrospect, how students interact within the educational process and our use of technology to assist in that process has been in flux since the early 1900s. Not so long ago in the one-room schoolhouse, students used slates and chalk to document their individual responses and to practice instructional content ranging from spelling to grammar to mathematic computation and problem solving. For the most part, education has evolved significantly since that time and has undergone a profound and significant technological revolution. I would like to suggest that in education, "What is today's state-of-the-art is virtually obsolete tomorrow." And yet, what is the state-of-the-art of yesterday has actually been the foundation for the evolution of what will be the state-of-the-art in education tomorrow.

In my first year of education (1979), my (Werner's) supervising principal was appalled at the volume of paper teachers had to purchase to keep up with the mountains of worksheets they were duplicating for their students. He questioned whether or not the quality of direct instruction to students was being compromised through a daily reliance on "drill and practice worksheets" across subject areas. His two concerns were the rising cost of paper, and whether or not an overreliance upon this instructional strategy actually enhanced student performance. The principal at the time was sixty-nine years old and a product of early twentieth-century education.

Almost coincidental to his concern was his receipt of an educational catalog that highlighted a possible solution to an overreliance upon this instructional strategy. With a school of well over 360 students and an estimated prohibitive cost of paper and mimeograph supplies, he actually entertained the cost-effectiveness of purchasing slates and chalk for every student in the school. He reasoned these slates would reduce instructional supply costs, eliminate waste of materials, and require teachers to place a higher emphasis upon the quality of direct instruction.

In an unusual twist of fate, rather than going back to reliance upon "old-school strategies" due to budgetary constraints, this sage principal embraced new technological changes that included new high-speed analog copiers. Prior to this technological advance, the only actual copying machine available to the school was what was called a "thermal-fax copier." Although this machine was neither high speed nor high volume, it did allow for the reproduction of important documents and print ready mimeograph masters from which to make student worksheets. Very few people within the school had access to this machine and all use had to be approved by the principal. For this small rural school, rapid technological change was right around the corner.

With the school's first high-speed copier contract, a low-cost solution to high-speed, high-volume production was available to all schools. This technological innovation provided the principal with the ability to efficiently address student work production needs schoolwide across a variety of subject areas while providing the ability to monitor "worksheet" quality, instructional alignment, and daily volume of student materials. Teachers reluctant to relinquish their control over the production process and who were equally concerned about the monitoring of this process continued to secretly use old hand-crank and electric mimeograph machines to conceal how often and abundantly they used daily drill and practice worksheets.

Historically, in the face of change, some individuals may be more reluctant or experience more difficulty in learning new, more effective ways of accomplishing tasks. I (Deana), for instance, must shamefully concede that I had 148 voice mails on my cell phone. I had not bothered to learn how to retrieve my messages on my new phone and ignorance was bliss until my longtime friend called me, irate because I had not been returning her calls. You can bet that I promptly learned how to check my phone messages and did I get an earful! In education, as in all things, growth is necessarily accompanied by growing pains and resistance in the short run, only to be embraced as an integral, practical, and useful fact of life in the near future. Simply put, what is today's necessity will become what is referred to as "old-school" tomorrow. In our fast-paced society there is a saying that "if you buy something today that is the state-of-the-art, its replacement is already in production for you to purchase tomorrow." Thus, the practical principal must research and understand changes on the horizon, particularly in technology, to effectively assess its utility to the instructional process and maximize responsiveness to changes to improve instruction and student performance, while effectively managing funding resources to address these changes.

Not so many years ago, the first digital watch available to the public probably cost about $300. Today, a comparable timepiece can be purchased at any major discount store for about $5. In the early stages of any technological advance, the expense related to change in terms of research, development, and production is reflected in its price to the consumer. The first calculators available to the average consumer were exorbitantly costly and yet today, analogous to the watch, one can purchase a rather sophisticated calculator at the local store for well under $10. In the late 1950s, the most up-to-date computer was the Unisys mainframe used by the federal government. This computer was so large that it took up several floors of a federal building.

The computing capacity and utility of that computer can now be found in most of our home personal computers. With the advent of personal computers also came the ability to assist instruction through the use of terminals and personal computers by students and teachers, individually and in laboratory situations. In the mid-80s, my school purchased four TRS 80 personal computers. In the early days of personal computers, software availability and applications for student use were severely limited. The unlimited learning potential with the use of computers, however, was evident to the flexible administrator who embraced change. Without appropriate technical support or understanding, many schools went through "growing pains" in terms of the cost for software materials, additional computers, appropriate technological support, and assistance in their effective use. Thousands of dollars were spent on hardware and software, which were limited in their ability to engage students and effectively impact the quality of instruction or skill mastery in the students who used them. Nonetheless, a practical principal knows that for growth to occur, it has to start somewhere. When preparing to respond to changes on the horizon, a wise leader should make informed, effective decisions that are based upon deliberate research and evaluation as well as a well-thought-out plan for how that change should be managed for the purpose it is planned to address.

Technology will never completely replace effective teachers. Even though distance learning is being increased by leaps and bounds, we know at the other end of the computer in that particular course room is a certified teacher. As systems make more and more online courses available to students during the school year and through summer school, teachers may feel that their presence is no longer necessary. As long as we have human beings with human needs and emotions, a corresponding need will exist for human guidance, understanding, and facilitation of the educational process. Technological change and innovation will continue to offer the teacher a host of invaluable resources and tools to enhance and broaden the education of children today and in the future.

Many of the best practices of the one-room schoolhouse are still used today with extraordinary efficacy, freshness, and utility. The slates and chalk of yesterday are still seen today in our classrooms in the form of individual student "white boards" and dry erase markers; laptops can be transformed into virtual whiteboards too. The strategies for their use are essentially the same as they were yesterday, yet their current use continues to permeate instruction in most of our elementary classrooms today. This very strategy is cited by most as a "best practice" in engaging students and monitoring student work on a daily basis. It provides an instant assessment tool, a fun and engaging activity for students, and a cost-effective method of providing drill and practice activities, which will allow for the reuse of a nonconsumable resource repeatedly over time. The overhead projector of yesteryear has evolved to a computerized system of projector and laptop interfacing that allows the teacher to provide high-interest PowerPoint multimedia presentations with sights, sounds, and concepts attractively integrated to captivate the attention spans of today's youth.

Smart pads and other variations on individual student stations allow entire classrooms to work together with the teacher in facilitated interactions to master concepts and enhance learning. We must remember that today's best practices are directly tied back to those foundation strategies used by the schoolmarm in the one-room schoolhouses across our frontiers of our not-so-distant pasts. These strategies and practices are the effective precursors to those used by our current teachers striving to provide the "free and appropriate public education" that has become the institutional cornerstone of our great nation today.

A practical principal must manage effective instructional change, and with those changes the administrator must be alert to the pitfalls and dangers lurking ahead. Unforeseen difficulties may include unplanned, additional expenses; extensive training times; and traps the students might fall in. These days, students are very techno-savvy. Traversing the World Wide Web with little or no difficulty, students may move in and out of sites quickly without being readily detected. Their movements may not be easily tracked by a teacher who is not well traveled on the Internet highway. Student safety, viruses, pornography, and other serious issues arise when technology is not monitored closely.

The knowledgeable principal must also manage the impact and integration of technological innovation and change to effectively meet the instructional needs of the student of the future. Great principals plan for the effective evolution of appropriate instruction. They use their budgets and available resources to orchestrate a delicate blend of human and resource interaction to provide the best desired instructional outcomes possible across their student populations. Years ago as I read an educational journal, I came across a cartoon that was both prophetic and profound in its simplicity. It was a picture of a couple rather advanced in age, sitting at what appeared to be a kitchen table. In the center of the table was a black box with a glassy face and a few dials and buttons on the front of the box. The caption underneath it read, "Gee, it sure looks like a nice television, however, it has lousy reception, and I can't get it to work." The box in the picture was really a microwave. To me this simple cartoon summarizes how important it is for the practical principal to have an understanding of where education has been to have a vision for the future. We all know someone (Deana, perhaps) who uses their microwave oven to merely heat liquids or possibly warm something up to eat. We also know that there are those among us who can use a microwave to cook a roast or an entire meal with multiple entrées.

Practical principals realize the institution of education is in a constant state of flux, as are the ever-changing needs of the students we all serve. The schools of tomorrow will demand an effective and conscious positive movement from yesterday to today and from today throughout our futures. Great principals must be realistic visionaries with an understanding of how education got here and where education is going. Finally, in our opinion, the effective use and integration of technology will provide that very bridge which promises to connect the best practices of instructional personnel with the ever-changing needs of the institution of education to effectively meet the needs of the students of tomorrow.

Chapter Eleven

Budget: It Costs What?

Welcome to the big league. As the principal of the school, you have more than likely inherited the responsibility and awesome task of managing a multimillion dollar budget that supports the daily operation of a comprehensive educational center. The majority of this budget will include all fixed costs for daily operation, from salaries and benefits of employees to operational expenses for electricity, water, and other essential services. The budget will also be comprised of contractual obligations for leased products and services that may include copiers, consultations, product maintenance, and repairs. Principals have little to no control over the majority of their fixed costs.

Salaries of employees are generally determined by negotiated contracts with local unions, district policies and procedures, and other factors usually beyond the control of school principals. Much like a personal household budget, though, principals must be actively engaged in monitoring the school's expenditures on a daily basis. Thorough management allows the principal to be more effective in providing the best possible educational programs and experiences for students.

Although it is conceivable and likely that budgetary processes vary across districts and from one state to another, most school principals do have daily discretion to spend a portion of the funds allocated to their schools specifically to meet the goals and objectives determined and established by the local school stakeholders. Most school administrators are aware that the two easiest ways for principals to be fired or suffer legal consequence involve knowingly allowing harm to come to students or inappropriately handling the school's funds. Simply put, if one misuses, inappropriately manages, or misappropriates public funding that individual could lose his job, or even end up in jail. Now that we have gotten your attention, let's talk budgets.

Typically, principals rely upon their secretaries and bookkeepers to make sure all resources and services are paid for in the right fashion with the appropriate funds and with the proper approval. Some principals may even allow those experienced personnel to prepare the budget for the upcoming year and bring it to them for approval. Very frequently, principals are appointed lacking experience in dealing with a school system's budgetary process. The administrators, though, may have had specific training in the accounting process or in dealing with state funding. It is absolutely imperative that the practical principal be directly involved in the development and implementation of all phases of the school's budgetary process.

The practical principal must be involved in the budget process to assure that the school's staff can best meet its goals and objectives for students. Effective management of the school's budget implies that the principal understands and is driven by the vision and mission of the school. Such management must take into consideration system rules and regulations regarding funds. The practical principal will develop a strategic plan for how the budget can be appropriately expended to meet the school's needs and goals. Principals often receive informal, on-the-job budgetary training. In my (thank goodness this is Werner here; Deana has a tough time managing her personal budget) case, I was given the opportunity to review and proofread budget materials prior to becoming an administrator. Little did that secretary know (or maybe she did) that she was providing me with invaluable insight into the financial process for a school.

Initially, the school secretary would ask me to double-check her figures for accuracy and correctness. Within a couple of years, knowing that the principal was a manager who did not have a strategic plan in mind for the money, the secretary would allow me to make suggestions and assist her in the process of addressing future school needs through the budgetary process. Over time, I began to learn the specific functions and objects of the various accounts managed within the budget. I also began to understand that specific funds were only designated to pay for particular activities, resources, or services. Eventually, I understood how with much forethought, a new budget could be appropriately constructed to meet future program requirements and provide better services to the students and school staff. As educational programs and school accountability issues have evolved, so too has the demand for greater fiscal involvement, and budgetary understanding has correspondingly grown in the role of the school principal.

In my (Werner again) school system, roughly 85 percent of the individual school's budget is consumed in providing salaries and benefits for its employees. About another 10 percent of the school's budget is devoted to the general overhead that supports the daily operation of a school (i.e., water, electricity, routine maintenance, grounds upkeep, service contracts, and operational supplies). Given then that 95 percent of the school's budget is devoted to expenditures beyond the control of the school's principal, many would assume that very little money is left for the principal to be accountable for. Actually, that 5 percent represents a significant amount of money for a school's programmatic needs. With strategic planning and long-range understanding, those funds can go a long way to help a school be more responsive to its future and institutional needs.

During my last school assignment as principal, the school's annual operating budget was about $6.5 million. Thus, I had discretion to determine the appropriate expenditure under my direct control of about $350,000 annually. It's easy to see that without conscious reflection and strategic planning, considerable waste of funding could occur. The practical principal will routinely review expenditures to make certain monies are being spent appropriately.

Among these funds are federal monies for the provision of exceptional student education programs, Title I funds for the provision of compensatory education services for the school's children (based upon free- and reduced-lunch eligibility), and special funds provided through State or Federal grants earmarked to provide additional programs and services for the school's student population. In all of these cases, the practical principal must be capable of effectively budgeting and monitoring how these funds can be properly used to provide a wide continuum of materials, resources, and services that will improve the quality of instruction and program delivery.

Every district will have rules that govern how materials, resources, or services can be purchased to appropriately meet the needs of the school and its students. Principals may have discretion to allocate funds for supplies for teachers; school-based training initiatives; instructional materials; and for maintenance contracts with vendors and services. In the last school to which I was assigned, I inherited a situation wherein the previous principal did not clearly understand the budgetary process. The former administrator also failed to anticipate the additional budgetary liability that could be incurred through a contractual agreement and the subtleties of the contract's terms. The principal had entered into a five-year copier contract that included a monthly and an annual schoolwide copy limit. The school's faculty and staff were thrilled at the opportunity to use a high-speed, high-volume duplicating system to produce documents and worksheets for students. As with all copier lease agreements, there is a charge for each copy in excess of the allowable amount of copies per month. When negotiating a copier contract, it is good practice to ascertain the monthly production allowance to understand whether the terms of the contract are cost effective. Most copiers have an internal process that can be used to prevent excess use without approval. This process provides an internal protection for the lessee to avoid excess charges for exceeding the allowable monthly or quarterly copy count.

In the previous principal's case, this process was not clearly specified, understood, or implemented. In their enthusiasm, the staff had used the allowable copy capacity for the entire five-year period by the end of the first year. Although the school had consumed the entire copy capacity for a five-year period, it still had four years left to go on the lease of the copier. According to its contract, the school would continue to receive a bill for the use of the copier every month for the next forty-eight months, whether it was used or not. The problem was, however, if the school actually used the copier, it would be charged 8¢ per copy for every copy made. As a result, I inherited a school in which a brand-new copier sat unused in a closet for four years because the school's budget did not have sufficient funds available to pay for additional copy costs associated with the contract.

Today's principal can ill afford to misunderstand the terms of any contract for a good, service, or product. In this case, the previous principal had to implore the school system to provide them additional funding to enter into another copier contract to provide services for the school. A practical principal rarely wants to request special funding dispensation as a result of an error of omission or understanding. Such errors can be a poor reflection of business sense, fiscal judgment, and, ultimately, skills as an effective educational leader.

Principals may also have discretion to use school funds to assist in the maintenance of their facilities—to repair, renovate, and replace the infrastructure of the school as it decays or falls into disrepair over time. In addition, the principal may be able to allot funds for the purchase of additional equipment deemed important in maintaining the school and its grounds. Strategic use of school-based funds to provide efficient contracted services to maintain and repair the building or the school's equipment can often be more effective and responsive to school needs than relying upon district provided services. Most school systems have a systemwide maintenance department to assist with school repairs and maintenance. Depending upon the size of the district, the timing and effectiveness of the services provided by district maintenance departments may vary considerably. Over the years, I have learned district maintenance departments appreciate school principals who practice preventive maintenance and use their own discretionary funds to repair and maintain their facilities when possible.

A principal who establishes such a reputation within the district can often improve district responsiveness and assistance in helping with repair and maintenance issues when it is known he or she is positively and qualitatively involved in the upkeep of the school. Likewise, practical principals seek to connect and engage external stakeholders as partners in their efforts to deliver a quality program and improve their schools. Thus, an effective principal will establish and facilitate positive working relationships with district mainte-nance supervisors and maintenance personnel to provide services and support for the school. Principals must be realists and should understand how to ef-fectively engage other district employees in their efforts to improve their fa-cility. They must also be capable of determining when it is the appropriate time to use the district's assistance and support and when it may be more de-sirable to use the school's discretionary funds to address a school's needs.

Most school systems have some equitable way of providing school discre-tionary funding to purchase state-adopted textbooks and materials to be used in each subject area. Textbooks are among the most expensive materials pro-vided within our schools. Publishers also provide a rich menu of comple-mentary materials and resources to supplement instruction with the text-books. In the first adoption year of any textbook, quite a few ancillary materials are provided free of charge to comprehensively support the teach-ers' daily instructional efforts. The practical principal must carefully review each adopted textbook and its supplemental materials prior to purchase to un-derstand what will be provided free of charge and what will represent an ad-ditional exorbitant replacement cost from the school's textbook budget.

A rule of thumb here is that once you give teachers a material or resource that they feel is of great utility, the teachers will naturally want it replaced and maintained as long as they are using that textbook. Publishers take great care in aligning their materials with the district's instructional goals and objectives and the state's guidelines for instructional content. Companies also provide scripted teacher's guides and resources covering every aspect of support ma-terial imaginable to assist teachers. Most of these support materials tend to be consumable, which means once they are used they have to be replaced. When a teacher becomes dependent upon a consumable material that is considered to be an integral and vital piece of their instructional program for that content, the teacher will have an expectation of its replacement independent of the availability of funding to do so.

Textbooks and their accompanying publisher-provided support materials are analogous to a new automobile and the options one might choose to have added on in its purchase price. The textbook can be viewed as a base model, and the ancillary materials can be viewed as luxury options. The practical principal must carefully weigh the budget available for the purchase of these materials taking care not to be locked into an "extended warranty or fancy un-dercoat option" that may make the effective allocation of the school's text-book resources vastly more complicated.

The practical principal's pursuit of continuous quality improvement presumes the presence of long-range planning and an understanding of the instructional and curricular developmental needs of the school's student population. Additionally, practical principals must possess a cogent understanding of the instructional skill development needs of the school's faculty and staff to offer training in this area. The strategic use of the school's budget and resources available will assist the principal in providing responsive instructional programs and comprehensive training that improve the quality of instruction. For school-based budgeting to be an effective tool, a complete understanding of how students and teachers interact to achieve educational goals within the classroom and throughout the school is imperative. To insure a successful future for a school's instructional efforts, the cognizant principal must understand the needs and capabilities of the faculty and staff along with the wide range of materials and resources currently available to them. Viewed in this context, the effective use and implementation of the school's budget can make the difference between a school floundering in its instructional effort and one that epitomizes exemplary student and staff accomplishment.

Chapter Twelve

Maintenance:
Can I Ask The Custodians To Do This?

The physical environment of your school creates the foundation on top of which all daily instruction occurs. It can add to or detract from the ideal climate one seeks to provide and maintain for the students, parents, and staff of a school. The average person in their daily drive around the town can look at a school's exterior and grounds and fairly accurately imagine what kind of school it is based upon how well it is maintained. I (Deana) find that this is not necessarily true. I have worked at a couple of schools that had excellent faculties and many resource services available to students; however, the conditions of the school were horrible. Unfortunately, I have even had to work in a building day in and day out whose exterior was covered in bird droppings. I have had to put off going to the bathroom because of a roach problem in the teacher's bathroom. Also, I have had my gloved hand stuck on the sticky traps that I was trying to set out in an effort to quell the spider problem in one of my school offices.

One of the things that I (Werner) find remarkably interesting in my travels to different cities and counties throughout my state is the differences in how well schools are maintained. A huge difference might exist between the exterior appearances of a school in one district and that of a different school in another district. Certainly, resources, funding, and the age of the buildings have a lot to do with these variations. The appearance of the school, both inside and out, can be important determinants in the quality of the teaching that is provided and the learning that is experienced within a given school. Well-maintained schools can be found surrounded by dilapidated and decaying buildings in impoverished neighborhoods while schools with small cities of portables can be seen in extremely affluent neighborhoods.

What must it be like to be students within those classrooms? It is our firm belief that for children to learn effectively they must feel safe and comfortable while being taught daily in a pleasant environment conducive to learning. The way in which a facility is kept clean and maintained sets a tone for every activity that occurs within it. Principals cannot choose the age of the facility that they are assigned to, but they can maintain the facilities in the best possible condition for students, their families, and the faculty who inhabit them each and every day.

Depending on the demographic composition of the student population, school is the cleanest, most climate controlled, and most pleasant place those children will be on a daily basis. Every administrator has been in a classroom that was devoid of cheer with basically four walls, some desks, a chalkboard, and people interacting within it. Within the very same building, every administrator will find a similar classroom constructed the same way as the previous room that is a virtual garden of learning due to the creative way the teacher has decorated and maintained it. The difference between two such rooms in the same building is a focus upon what that room means for children and how it is maintained. We have worked in school buildings that were over sixty years old and school buildings that were brand new. We have been in older schools that had clean, cheerful, well-maintained classrooms, and have been in newer schools in which the classrooms were unkempt and deteriorating.

Both types of schools had an appropriate complement of custodial personnel and resources with which to maintain them. The only difference between the two was their leadership's resolve and focus upon their adequate maintenance. The physical care and upkeep of the school helps create and maintain the emotional and physical attachment or connectedness all stakeholders have for that school. The practical principal has the opportunity to create a sense of community with the attention paid to the school's upkeep and maintenance. Inattention to a school's surroundings may result in a sense of disconnection, alienation, and fragmentation of positive school culture. For schools to succeed in their mission with students, it is absolutely essential that students and staffs share a sense of personal connection to the school's physical environment. Great principals want their schools to be safe, warm, and inviting places in which their staffs and students can work productively together to accomplish their shared mission and vision. The key to accomplishing these goals is the active involvement of a transformational leader who recognizes the interrelatedness of all factors influencing school operation and actively engages in monitoring their interaction so they complement and reinforce one another.

A practical principal must have a keen understanding of the capabilities of the custodial/maintenance staff assigned to the school. Some schools have been blessed with staffs with tremendous work ethics and maintenance skill backgrounds. Others have hard-working staffs that basically have to have their working lives scheduled almost on a minute-by-minute basis. For a principal new to the school, weeks or months of personal observation and assessment may be needed to determine the strengths and challenges of the school's maintenance or custodial staff. Years ago, when I (Werner) worked for a previous principal, I observed him spending the better part of an academic school year trying to help the custodial staff become more efficient at properly cleaning all the school's classrooms. Although he knew very little about what they actually did when they cleaned a classroom, he soon developed a cleaning schedule that specified how much time they should spend daily in each classroom.

Many custodians follow directions very literally. Schedules rarely allow for an individual who is eager to maintain a schedule to deal with something unexpected or not previously suggested as an appropriate cleaning activity. As the weeks went by, the principal continued to get complaints from teachers that this custodian or that one did not sweep underneath the desk or rinse scouring powder out of a sink. He would get reports that insect droppings were not wiped off of windowsills. Of course, each time the principal received a complaint, he met with the head custodian to discuss the issue. In almost every case, the argument was that the schedule did not allow enough time for custodians to pay sufficient attention to these little unforeseen details.

On one occasion, the head custodian said he thought he had a way of addressing the problem, but it would require changing the schedule. The principal was adamant that the schedule needed to be maintained; therefore, it could not be changed. Almost weekly, there would be more complaints from different teachers often regarding the various custodians. Finally, almost in disgust, the principal suggested replacing one or more of the other custodians. The head custodian continued to suggest that his workers were very conscientious, but they just could not get these little details taken care of while continuing to adhere to the principal's schedule. In desperation, the administrator decided to permit the head custodian to develop an alternate schedule.

The head custodian then met with his personnel to discuss all the recent complaints and the work they were doing. After several conversations, appealing to their sense of pride in their work, he established a cleaning routine that gave them flexibility to focus on details instead of interpreting the schedule literally. Born out of this discussion evolved a process which paid attention to details, while being loosely governed by some timeline parameters in completing the custodians' daily work in the rooms assigned to them. Teacher complaints became almost nonexistent. Many began treating the custodian as a partner in maintaining their classroom environments, and actually became open to suggestions on how each could work together more effectively. The end result was that classroom environment improved throughout the school, teacher satisfaction in custodian performance improved, and custodians began to see that their efforts were recognized as vitally important to the success of the school.

Issues vary from school to school when it comes to the maintenance and upkeep of the facility. What may be a custodial problem in one school may not surface in another. During one of my principalships, I was assigned to a school that was very rural (located near a national forest). The school was roughly forty-five miles from district maintenance support and was many miles from the nearest town or community. It had a rather large retention pond surrounded by a fence, approximately ten acres of property on its grounds, and was one of the newest schools within the district. I was immediately struck by how clean and well kept the facility and grounds appeared. It did not take me very long to recognize that the school had an excellent custodial staff who took great pride in maintaining the school's appearance inside and out. One of the custodians was very mechanically inclined and had worked extremely hard over the years to keep all of the equipment operational.

Most of the school's vacuum cleaners, lawnmowers, and various other pieces of groundskeeping equipment were outdated. When I asked the staff why these things had not been replaced, the reply was, "the school didn't have any funds to replace them." Upon review of the school's comprehensive budget, I discovered tens of thousands of dollars of the school's discretionary maintenance budget had not been utilized over the preceding three years. Custodians had been advised by their previous principals to make do with the equipment they had with the hope that the system would eventually replace what was not working. School custodians and maintenance staffs must be provided with suitable tools to perform their jobs effectively. For years, this particular staff kept their equipment going on a wing and a prayer, only consuming maintenance funds to pay for repairs they absolutely could not do on their own. School leaders had given no consideration for equipment depreciation or even an understanding of the effective lifespan of a piece of equipment. As mechanical instruments began to fail, the staff was less productive in maintaining the facility and its grounds.

A practical principal must strive to provide every employee with the appropriate tools to effectively perform their tasks if the utmost quality of their work is to be realized. The school had spent thousands of dollars repairing vacuum cleaners and lawn equipment in excess of the cost of their actual replacement. The practical principal must always seek the most cost-effective way to provide materials, equipment, and resources necessary to adequately support the school's staff in the performance of their daily duties to maintain a physical environment that is pleasant and conducive to sustained learning.

As stakeholders in the success of the school, teachers often do their part in making certain the school looks its best. Sometimes their efforts may come unexpectedly and in unusual ways as teachers gain assistance from the maintenance staff to improve the physical environment of the school. I (Deana) have even been called upon to make my well-known "decadent brownies" for the system maintenance staff for making, not one, but two bathrooms handicapped accessible for a new student. Now the staff members would have performed those duties anyway, but certainly the brownies went a long way in letting them know how much I appreciate what they do for me in an effort to serve the students who are not always able to express their gratitude.

As an administrator, Werner experienced a case wherein a couple of classroom teachers indicated a desire to have their classrooms painted. They knew a work order to the district maintenance department might take six months or longer to get the job done. According to district procedure, the teachers were also aware that their rooms would only be painted in the same drab color they had been painted fifteen years previously. One of the young educators knew a couple of men at the maintenance department personally. As the year drew to an end, she came to the principal requesting permission to paint the rooms along with another teacher. The teacher also queried if the pair could visit her friend in the district maintenance department to determine how long it would take for a work order to be completed. With the administrator's permission, the two teachers decided to drop by the maintenance department during the summer before their trip to the Florida beach.

Dressed in bikinis and scant cover-ups, these two attractive teachers went to the maintenance department, asked directions to the paint shop, and went to visit the painters. One can imagine the hubbub this impromptu visit created among the maintenance workers. Of course, the staff was more than willing to be of service to the educators. In fact, both of the classrooms were painted in the colors of their choice within a two-week time period. By the way, I took quite a good deal of ribbing from my principal friends and the maintenance department because they all believed I had put the teachers up to this strategy to get something done for a school independent of process and policy. Had I been an accomplished practical principal at the time, I may have foreseen this incident occurring. Regardless of our protests and denials, many of my colleagues still believe I am not beyond stretching the limits of protocol to get something done. As an unintended positive side effect of this event, whenever a work order was put in by my school, we almost always received a prompt response promptly accompanied by a visit from the appropriate maintenance workers desiring to help us address the issue in question.

In conclusion, a practical principal must understand the capabilities of the school's maintenance and custodial staff. Dynamic practical principals should effectively utilize a blend of school and district funds to maintain the school's facilities and grounds to provide the highest quality of physical learning environments possible for the school. The principal addressing equipment and staff challenges must utilize the school's budget to contract for services and maintenance assistance when the school staff is unable to or incapable of providing them as those needs are identified. Efficient principals understand the importance of a well-maintained facility in establishing and supporting the best learning environments possible. It is far easier to maintain a pleasant and effective learning environment over time than it is to repair one that is in a sad state of disrepair. Likewise, it is more cost effective to engage in preventive maintenance and ongoing positive upkeep than it is to renovate and repair something that has been neglected over time. Finally, the practical principal knows every stakeholder within the school needs to be connected to the vision and mission established by the school to assure those broad goals will be accomplished. Every student, every parent, and every staff member, regardless of their specific role or function, can and should feel they are an important part of the organization.

Chapter Thirteen

School Climate: Is It Chilly In Here?

Most people would agree that within minutes of walking onto the school grounds or into a classroom itself, our innate human barometer will automatically gauge the temperature of the setting. Such perceptions (or misperceptions) will be based on a number of factors including observations of the quality of human interactions within the school. The physical surroundings also influence our perceptions along with a host of other environmental variables such as the décor of the classrooms and common areas in the school, the ease of mobility throughout the school, and the demeanor of the students and staff.

For lack of a better description, this perceptual reading can be referred to as the school's climate. A school can have a climate that is conducive to learning and mutual interactive relationships within its walls or it can have a climate that virtually destroys the morale of everyone on campus. Much has been written recently about the importance of creating and maintaining a "single-minded school culture" within our schools today. The culture of the school is an expression of the quality of the climate that exists within it. A healthy school climate fosters growth and allows positive alliances to form among all the stakeholders within the school. The climate is a vitally important element that affects the goals and purposes of the school.

If we are to believe that the three R's of education as an institution of the twenty-first century are to be "rigor, relevance, and relationships;" then the quality of the relationships established in the schools must be the foundation upon which an effective school culture and school climate are built. We believe the single most powerful indicator of a school's success involves the quality of the relationships existing within them. Within educational settings, it is therefore suggested that where positive relationships and bonds exist between teachers and students, an aggregate single-minded culture will emerge that will actually raise the ceiling on what can be mutually achieved together by the group as a whole. Embracing these ideals, the practical principal's role then becomes that of effectively tapping the endless potentials of students and staff members.

How can a principal be equal to such a lofty task? The answer is quite a paradox because it is both complex and simple. To create a school culture and climate that generates the highest achievement, a practical principal must possess an unparalleled combination of talents and understanding of the school's developmental process and its future destination. To obtain such knowledge, the practical principal must delve into researching the nuances of the school, forge strong ties among staff members, and develop a realistic action plan for the future.

Every administrator at some point has used interview questions in the selection of a new teacher. The Gallup Association has a selection instrument that is called Teacher-Perceiver that is generally considered an effective tool in the hiring process. One particular question in this instrument addresses a central issue of what is one of the most important traits of an effective teacher. The question asks, "What do you have to do to get students excited about learning?" The answer is you have to be excited about teaching. If we extend this idea to a question that would be helpful in selecting school leadership candidates, the question would be, "What do you have to do to get teachers excited about teaching?" Certainly, the answer should involve excitement about leading. To be an effective leader, the school principal must exhibit a "passion, commitment, and spirit" that is palpable and discernible to every stakeholder within the school.

The cornerstone of an effective school culture and climate involves a passionate, committed, and spirited leader who can effectively articulate the strengths and challenges the school faces, the vision and mission of their common purpose, and the proposed pathway they must travel together to achieve success in the future. A practical principal must be a catalyst for change while nurturing all stakeholders throughout their journey in moving forward to effectively address the needs of the students of the future. Several years ago, I (Werner) was assigned to a school in which the previous principal believed his role one of stewardship. He was an effective manager of the status quo in maintaining what he believed to be an enduring institution centered around unchanging routines, rituals, and ideals. His fundamental belief was that he should manage resources, maintain and enforce student discipline, and replicate the same pattern of instruction and interaction among the staff from one year to the next.

His having well over forty years of experience in education, the experienced administrator had seen new programs come and go, resources and funds shift from scarcity to abundance, and literally thousands of students proceed in and out of his institution throughout the years. He saw his role as maintaining consistency and predictability in an otherwise uncertain world. Although student populations and issues changed over time, he was most comfortable implementing the same formulaic educational response to their needs as long as he was the principal of that school. I can honestly say that he genuinely cared for children and he truly loved his school and the institution of education. What he lacked, in my opinion, was an ability to be responsive to the ever-changing needs of students and the ever-changing demands our society places on education to meet those needs.

The climate that evolved under his watch was one in which teachers went about doing their jobs day to day in whatever way they felt was useful, without guidance to be responsive to the growing needs of their student population. In such a climate, staff members truly resist change, fear it, and are hard-pressed to be effectively responsive to it when such change is imposed upon them by external authorities. The challenge for me as a school leader was to bring new "passion, commitment, and spirit" to the principalship of that school. I had to ignite the "purpose, passion, and potential" of the staff and students of the school to welcome change and move forward to address our combined needs and goals together. Practical principals must not only "talk the talk"; they must also "walk the walk."

The practical principal's role in regulating the climate of the school is critical. I (Deana) have had the unfortunate experience of working with school bullies. I am not just referring to students, but teachers who seek to intimidate children and adults. The level of animosity that such intimidation can create is oppressive. The climate of the school is affected by the attitudes, morale, and emotional ties engendered by the staff and students. When the climate is threatened by negative comments, repeated browbeating, gossip, and misinformation, school leaders must be able to adjust the conditions by redirecting the focus to a more positive light. Just as menacing faculty members can jeopardize the school climate, rigid or harsh rules also impede the development of a healthy climate.

The practical principal must help to align the passion inherent in all teachers with the mission they hope to address and accomplish together. Effective principals assist their students and staff in developing a culture that is not only defined by its purpose, but is also expressed in the pursuit of that purpose. When an engaged principal exudes excitement about school, the staff and students begin to experience it as well. They feel included, involved, and vital to their combined pursuit of accomplishments. The reason people are resistant to change is because they inherently believe they cannot be equal to the task. They believe for whatever reason the cards are markedly stacked against them. The practical principal must seek ways to establish and reinforce effective composite relationships among all stakeholders to help them recognize that achieving their combined goals is possible, probable, and easily within their reach.

When a single-minded school culture emerges that is based upon effective and facilitative relationships, the achievement of making a positive, qualitative difference in the lives of all students becomes an all-encompassing and driving force in the daily efforts of every stakeholder. This kind of commitment among stakeholders is not one that can be legislated through the power of the position. In other words, groups of people do not move toward a common direction simply because they are told to do so by a higher authority (a person with a position or title). All of us are obviously aware of the status, rank, authority, and responsibility implied in the position of a school principal. In management literature, the implication of that type of power is derived from a position or title called "position power." The leader who operates predominantly from a base of position power must rule with an iron fist armed with rules, regulations, and consequences for compliance or noncompliance.

A principal who operates using their status or title in the school's daily operation of the school or directives severely limits his efficacy and ability to help a school adapt to change. The climate and culture resulting from such leadership is stifling and formidable even though it can create some degree of success toward the achievement of certain common goals. The practical principal understands that "personal power" and its effective use is the key to successful endeavors when orchestrating human interactions to meet and exceed the demands of common challenges while striving to reach extraordinary goals together. Personal power is the innate human ability of an individual to inspire, motivate, and ignite the human potential within others to accomplish common goals. It is assumed that most people who pursue a career in public education do so because they are motivated by a sense of commitment to others and a strong desire to make a positive difference in the lives of children. It stands to reason that if a principal utilizes personal power properly, the effective use and articulation of those powers of persuasion can ignite and maintain that spark within the teachers, students, parents, and community members.

Ten percent of what can be achieved can be realized through the use of position power. It has also been said 90 percent of the good that can be accomplished when moving people toward a common goal can be achieved through the effective use of personal power. The implications of position power versus personal power should be obvious to the reader. We refer to the field of the effective use of personnel to accomplish group endeavors together as the field of human resources. Human beings are resources that, when properly motivated and inspired, can accomplish virtually any task together. Because human beings have different personalities, possess innate and differing abilities, and have free will and thought, the practical principal must be adept in reaching every individual within the school community to move in a positive fashion toward the achievement of common goals. Every action, memorandum, direction, and detail expressed in the principal's daily interactions with others within the school has far-reaching consequences upon the school's climate and culture. The practical principal holds these convictions and utilizes them to create and maintain a high-performing, highly rewarding school climate and culture.

Thus, the practical principal must follow these fundamental caveats to assist in the development and nurturance of strong positive relationships within the school for a healthy school culture and climate to exist. A practical principal must be extremely visible throughout the school, visiting classes and walking about the grounds, and must be seen in virtually every ancillary place within the school showing interest, involvement, and total quality immersion in the school's daily activities. Effective principals understand the curricular programs of the school and are actively engaged in professional conversations, trainings, and planning sessions concerning the development of instruction. Counselors are also valuable partners in fostering a strong school culture and healthy climate. Both Werner and I have actually had teachers tell us that it is hard to find us in our offices, because we are so involved in and about the school. It is quite a complement for an administrator to be viewed as a "doer" rather than a steward.

The practical principal should have emotional intelligence as well as social interactive understanding to take the pulse of the school to facilitate sound decisions and reinforce positive relationships. An effective principal handles disciplinary measures in a manner that leaves students and staff members with their dignity and respect. Collegial conversations with employees in the principal's office will be conducted not from behind the desk but next to the employee to create an atmosphere of openness and acceptance. These types of situations encourage and reinforce a positive climate and culture that unifies staff members and students as they work toward a common goal.

In conclusion, the practical principal should maintain an "open door policy" wherein students, parents, and staff members are able to enter and express themselves in a safe and accepting environment. A few days before this chapter was finished, I (Werner) was contacted by telephone by a former teacher who had worked at one of my schools. As a human resources director for the school system, she was seeking my assistance in obtaining recertification. Due to an impending move, the teacher was seeking to expedite the process.

A couple of minutes into the conversation she appeared to recognize my voice. After exchanging some pleasantries and completing our conversation regarding the recertification issue, she asked if she could pay me a complement. She indicated that when it came to students, teachers, and parents, I seemed to have had an uncanny ability to always do the right thing (even when there were those who disagreed with my decisions). She also commented on the culture and climate within the school, noting that it was the best she had ever enjoyed in her twenty-five years of teaching experience.

One could imagine how humbling this validation was for me. What even made the validation more poignant was the fact that this teacher was not particularly one of my best teachers. In the three years we worked together, I had to assist her with several negative parent interactions in which she was at fault. I even had to change her grade-level assignment and remove her from being chairperson of the grade level she was previously assigned in my first year at that school. She later relocated with her family when her husband was transferred to another county and thus we had lost track of each other for several years. I am telling this story to illustrate a point. We may never truly be aware of the influence we have on others until someone tells us of this impact, in many cases years later.

As difficult and challenging as this teacher was, I found a way to be respectful, preserve her dignity, and relate to her professionally in all of my dealings with her. She advised me that I had notably displayed my passion about school and my great concern for others. Although I never expected confirmation from such a teacher, I was truly humbled and rewarded to know my efforts were genuinely perceived and appreciated. The practical principal must always strive to create and reinforce those meaningful connections that build and validate enduring relationships that will lead to the greatest good for the largest number in every interaction within the school. As a practical principal, you set the stage for the school climate and culture, so remember to "always love what you do and not forget why you do it" (Gilliland 2005).

Chapter Fourteen

School Safety:
Who Is Minding the Children?

Whenever a principal is called upon to make a public statement about an event that occurred at the school that threatened student safety, the principal most certainly will remind parents that "our primary and foremost concern is the safety and well-being of our students." Before any meaningful instruction can occur within a school, the students must feel safe at school. In fact, feeling safe at school is one of the five factors associated with school connectedness, those strong school ties that serve to protect youth from risky behaviors. From arriving safely to school to walking through the adequately supervised halls and attending classes within a safe, secure facility, students must feel safe to learn, to connect to school, and to want to stay in school. Nurturing classrooms are part of the equation that can create an atmosphere for learning, but students must feel protected within the school walls.

Principals must have school safety and contingency plans for evacuating the buildings in the event of a wide range of situations that may arise unexpectedly. The classroom teacher must prepare and train students in a wide range of self-preservation and egress plans designed to contend with sudden emergencies. Among these are fire drills, tornado drills, intruder alerts or lockdowns, bomb threats, and total school evacuation to a secure location. The practical principal must be adept in communicating to the parents of students the depth and detail of potential threats to the safety and health of the students in an accurate, reassuring, and informative manner. Among all of the challenges facing today's principals, incidents threatening the health and safety of students are foremost concerns.

Administrators conduct drills to help school staff and students practice and rehearse how various occurrences will be handled.

In my (Deana's) neck of the woods, tornado drills are taken very seriously. The threat of severe weather can bring about panic in this area due to so many who have experienced the destruction firsthand. Managing mass egress during a time of confusion and alert requires efficient planning, training of all participants, and frequent practice. Most schools have within each of their classrooms, cafeterias, media centers, and ancillary rooms posted exit routes and procedures to be used for various emergencies. In many cases, primary and secondary egress routes are posted, which allow alternatives to evacuation in case a route may direct children into harm's way. Effective school systems require their principals to practice emergency procedures on a regular basis with notice to staff members of their occurrence in advance.

It is not unusual for a principal who has scheduled a fire drill to find during its implementation that either students or staff members or both failed to follow posted procedures for unusual reasons. Pre-kindergarten teachers might suggest that practices be postponed during nap time because it is hard to get the children up and organized on such short notice. Even in a scheduled situation with teachers properly notified of a fire drill, students might exit their classrooms without their shoes on because the teacher asked them to remove them prior to a nap.

A practical principal knows that if an emergency occurs, it will not necessarily happen at the most convenient moment in the day for the students and staff. On other occasions, teachers might fail to participate in the drills because they are so engrossed in instruction and they do not want to lose the teachable moment. Regardless of the rationalization or explanation, students and staff must at a moment's notice be prepared to cooperate in an activity that is designed to preserve their lives during an unexpected threatening event. Quite frankly, sometimes the school fire alarm experiences a short or mechanical anomaly, which creates an unexpected event. A true test of the school's ability to effectively evacuate its room comes during these moments when a principal can actually see who and how many staff members properly respond to the unexpected alert.

The effective principal will use these unexpected, nonthreatening events as a true test of the evacuation plans and procedures and will make adjustments accordingly. On one occasion, my (Werner's) staff was so well trained that when an unexpected alert occurred, even the teacher who was away from her children using the restroom in the teacher's lounge immediately left the porcelain stool and the restroom with her clothing around her ankles as she exited the building. Although this was a literal and startled response, in retrospect, it showed her desire to follow procedure and immediately get to a safe place with her children. I must admit, this event provided quite a chuckle among the staff after the fact.

Among the situations that create additional concern for principals are bomb threats and intruder alerts. These scary situations have only been punctuated by recent events in which students and staff members were shot or taken hostage during crisis situations. The frequency of such occurrences has demanded detailed planning and procedures be put in place and practiced to prepare for such eventualities. The practical principal can ill afford to ignore the suggestion of a possible intruder or explosive device in the school. Many times telephone threats or handwritten notes suggest the possibility of such an event, even detailing the time and location of the threat. During a bomb threat, buildings must be evacuated, law enforcement notified, and buildings methodically searched. Throughout the search process, students must be fully supervised in a safe area away from the building regardless of the time required for the search or the environmental conditions that exist outside of the building (i.e., snow, rain, or extremes of temperature).

There is no more frightening a threat than that of a dangerous intruder in the school. All personnel must be capable at a moment's notice of locking the school down and maximizing the safety of everyone in the building when alerted to such an event. Teachers must be prepared to lead students to the safest place in their rooms, away from windows and doors, and to remain there for the duration of the perceived threat. Due to the growing threat of violence on school campuses, schools must plan for such an event and practice the procedures to handle various scenarios. Simulations such as these assure the practical principal of the greatest attention to detail and a maximum opportunity to save lives should a real event unexpectedly materialize. No principal ever desires to have an intruder armed or otherwise on the campus.

These situations can arise as a result of an angry or hostile parent coming to school to make good a threat upon a staff member or employee, can be an unintended result of law-enforcement's attempt to apprehend a criminal in flight, or can be the result of the deliberate plan of a disaffected individual to do intentional harm to as many persons as possible, choosing the school itself as an opportunistic victim. The practical principal must be ever vigilant and prepared to expect the unexpected. A recent incident at my (Deana's) son's high school involved the possibility of imminent danger from friends of a disgruntled student. Apparently, the friends sent a text message advising the student that they were going to bring a gun to my son's school to settle the conflict. The student's girlfriend informed administrators and word traveled fast throughout the school. Frightened teens took out their cell phones and began calling parents to come get them. Alarmed parents, including myself, who received word from their own teenagers or other parents wanted to rush to rescue the children. It was especially difficult for me as the mother of an only child and a professional in the field to not be certain if my son was safe from harm. Although schools are supposed to be safe places, we are all well aware that danger lurks everywhere and that the schoolhouse is far from immune to violence that can take the lives of our children in an instant.

Luckily, no one brought a gun to the school and the matter was resolved relatively quickly, but not without some disquieted reflection on the part of administrators, parents, and community members. Some local school leaders were quick to blame the use of cell phones for the situation spiraling out of control with worried parents clamoring at the school doors demanding answers. Since the horrific tragedy at Columbine High School and the subsequent bloodshed in schools across the country, I personally do not want my son to be without a cell phone. That phone might serve as his only lifeline in a world and, yes, school, that can unfortunately be cruel, unyielding, and dangerous to the very innocent.

Now my son himself can be a force to be reckoned with, towering almost a foot over my head and weighing almost 150 pounds more than my petite frame, but he is no match for the barrel of a gun, other forms of violent weapons, or bombs. The acts of terrorism in this country have also heightened our awareness of the frailty of life as we go about our daily routines. Cell phones allow us to stay connected with our families and friends in a world filled with uncertainty. The dissemination of misinformation, though, can wreak havoc in the school. Hysteria among students, staff, and parents is something that school administrators want to avoid at all costs. The use of emergency notification systems wherein all parents are automatically notified in case of school closings or other occurrences can alleviate some, but not all, problems for the practical principal. The practical principal must be mindful of dangers from within and outside the school building. Across this country, many children stay away from school due to the very real threat of bullying on the campus.

Students can fall prey to bullies, sexual assaults, or other violent acts; therefore, the school leaders must safeguard against these offenses as much as possible. Preventive measures are much more effective than reactive, after-the-fact responses; however, the practical principal must have a plan in place if an incident does occur and prepare both students and staff with strategies that provide for their ultimate safety regardless of the threat. Schools adopt and utilize procedures for maintaining the safety and well-being of their students during tornadoes, hurricanes, snowstorms, and other weather events.

They must also be ever vigilant of public health threats as mundane as head lice or as serious as a threat of communicable diseases (i.e., various viruses, meningitis, measles, chickenpox, tuberculosis, and others). A practical principal must not only have knowledge of the appropriate responses to these risks, but must also be capable of effectively communicating these threats to public health officials, families of students, and the community at large while maintaining an objective, professional, and reassuring approach. Effective principals understand and implement appropriate procedures on a daily basis, in cooperation with district, law enforcement, public health, and civil response personnel. For the practical principal, the safety and well-being of the school's staff and students is not only a primary concern, it is a daily imperative. With preparation, articulation, and practice, every principal will hopefully be able to maintain an effective, safe environment in which students and staffs can work together to achieve their utmost educational success, unfettered by danger throughout the school year.

Chapter Fifteen

Final Thoughts at the End of the Day: From "MGT" to "TLC"

The recurring theme throughout this book has been the importance of connecting every stakeholder in a positive qualitative way to reach the school's goals and the higher purposes it seeks to achieve. In today's fast-paced and fragmented society, human beings often feel alienated from one another and detached from a higher sense of purpose connecting them all. The last bastion of social connectedness that preserves hope for a brighter future for everyone is the institution of public education primarily sustained in our schoolhouses throughout the nation. To the extent that effective relationships are created and maintained between all stakeholders within the school, extraordinary accomplishments are not only possible, but within our reach.

The public has a vested interest in the maintenance and conservation of our public schools that help to develop children's capabilities to meet and exceed the demands of the needs of the future. Protecting such a valuable social foundation is a noble and ideal goal. For our society to grow and flourish while providing our children with opportunities to realize their dreams in the not-too-distant future, the school administrator of tomorrow must be more than a steward of that institution. The practical principal must be a forward-thinking visionary in the development and growth of those opportunities. The days of the "Manager Steward" serving as the custodian of a stable and unchanging process has long passed.

The paradigm has shifted and we suggest that the role of the principal has unfolded into a guide and catalyst for meeting and exceeding the ever-changing educational needs of our students and schools. If public education is to evolve over time, the practical principal must transition from the "management" (MGT) of routines and rituals toward making a "Transformational Leadership Commitment" (TLC) in carrying out daily activities with all

95

stakeholders within the school. Such a move is critical for the principal to give everyone the assurance that the school leader is equal to the task ahead.

Historically, the three R's of educational management have involved maintaining and replicating the "routines, rituals, and reporting" encompassing all student instructional efforts within our schools. The daily activities of traditional managerial school principals included scheduling; budgeting; overseeing and evaluating employees; conducting fire drills and bus evacuations; student meals; student discipline; completing required reporting for district, state, and federal entities; maintaining the school site; and monitoring all phases of daily school operation. In its most conventional sense, the school has been an institution that has been replicated and reinforced over time to provide for the appropriate education of society's children. While guided by the same fundamental ideals, what we have come to view as an appropriate educational process has been subtly adjusted over the past one hundred years.

We all understand the magnitude of public school's noble obligation to provide a "free and appropriate public education" to every child, regardless of race, color, creed, handicap condition, cognitive ability, or economic circumstance. As society and the educational needs of our student populations change, our schools must also transform themselves to effectively respond to these changes. In his books, *Inventing Better Schools, Creating Great Schools,* and *Schools for the 21st Century,* noted author and educator Dr. Phillip Schlechty suggests that traditional educational process and public education as an institution have been tweaked about as far as possible in doing the things the way we have always done them while expecting to get improved results (Schlechty 2003; 1990; 2005). Dr. Schlechty notes that we have practiced routines, rituals, and traditional approaches to a point where we have reached diminishing returns in providing the best educational opportunities possible while supposedly being responsive to students' evolving needs (Schlechty 2003). Simply put, relying upon traditional school structures and processes has obtained "about as much water out of that rock" as we in education can expect to get (Schlechty 2003). Dr. Schlechty suggests we should reinvent our schools to create more responsive institutions adept to the numerous changes in society and student needs (Schlechty). Public educators must also anticipate societal changes in the future. The practical principal of tomorrow must, therefore, become a "transformational leader" who is committed to leading the charge of public education's evolution to respond to the multiple needs of today's students.

Anyone who has been involved in public education within the past twenty years has observed a rapid transformation within our society directly attributable to rapid advances in technology. Within the past 150 years, society has evolved from an agrarian to an industrial to a fast-paced technological society. As a result, many challenges have arisen to the ways in which we teach and in the way in which students learn. Student populations have changed dramatically, thereby multiplying the factors that complicate the public education process. The instructional activities that normally engaged children in the classrooms of yesteryear are no longer effective in maintaining current student interest. In this fast-paced world of drive-through windows and television commercials embedded with multisensory stimuli, today's student learner must be "edu-tained" to ensure instructional content mastery.

Student learners now appear to have by nature shorter attention spans and a need for multisensory, multimodal instruction to maintain active engagement in all learning activities. In addition, rapid population shifts within our nation have created poverty zones in which employment opportunities for parents and high school graduates are almost nonexistent. Outsourcing of jobs to third world countries and technological innovation have made labor-intensive occupations a thing of the past. As a nation, we are on the precipice of a national crisis of unemployment or underemployment that will necessarily place greater demands on education and alter the demographic challenges inherent in the students of tomorrow. Again, these factors will markedly change what students must learn to be successful tomorrow and how we effectively educate them in our classrooms today. With the emergence of the computer and "virtual schools," the schoolhouse of tomorrow will be entirely different from those structures that currently exist. Educators can no longer afford "to keep doing what we have always done" and continue to be surprised that we keep getting the same results.

The transformational school principal of tomorrow must be capable of assessing the status of the school and its educational programs in the here and now while planning to meet the changing needs of students in the future. The practical transformational principal will assist the faculty and staff in effectively utilizing current best practices and approaches while modifying and adjusting them to be appropriately responsive to educational changes on the horizon. Such principals will seize each moment to help every stakeholder find an appropriate role and functional place within the school and its learning community. Practical principals must not only have a passion for what they do, but they must also effectively radiate that enthusiasm for learning to maximize the educational experience for everyone in the school. A transformational leader will recognize the special qualities and abilities that make an individual teacher the best choice to help a previously unsuccessful, unmotivated, and disaffected learner develop into a student who achieves academic, social, and emotional success. We have all known students perceived as troublemakers and nonlearners who experienced success and stepped out of a failing mold when provided access to a highly skilled and nurturing teacher. The practical principal must know how to orchestrate and guide such successful educational experiences. Practical principals can also reach faculty members through professional development to help them grow, stretch, and become better teachers.

The practical principal of the future is one who will possess skills, knowledge, and understanding that build confidence, the capacity for growth, and the appropriate commitment among all stakeholders. The effective leader can and should be the bridge between tradition and impending change to create, mold, and nurture a school that itself endures and transforms to effectively respond to this change over time. To the extent that every human being within the schoolhouse feels included and believes each individual is a vital and essential part of that living and breathing entity which we call the school, unlimited human potentials can be achieved and realized by one and all. Everyone within the schoolhouse, no matter how minor or large the part, plays an integral role in the success of the school. From the parent to the food service worker, from the custodian to the teacher, from the support personnel to the principal, and to the very students themselves, everyone has a passion and purpose that can be ignited, motivated, and sustained by the practical principal.

Relating to these thoughts at the end of the day, a funny story comes to mind. One day a mother came into the school office obviously irritated and shouting as she came through the door. The first person to see her was the receptionist. Without losing a breath, the parent continued a tirade about her child's teacher and some perceived injustice she believed the teacher allowed to occur. As she came through the door, her three children trailed briskly behind her. A couple of parents, students, and several other school personnel were in the office when this angry mother and her children arrived. Of course, everyone was privy to the tirade. The receptionist, calmly and patiently, asked her to lower her tone and allow her to assist her with her problem. The parent demanded to see the principal, seeking immediate redress including termination of the teacher.

Upon hearing the diatribe, another office employee immediately sought out the principal, bringing him to the office to address the problem. The principal, the parent, and her children went into his office to discuss the issue. After some time, the parent emerged with her children in quite a different frame of mind than that which she possessed when she first entered the school's main office. Following reassurance from the principal that her complaint would be investigated and proper resolution would be suggested, the parent had calmed down and was proceeding out of the office. On her way out, she stopped to speak with the receptionist. She began to thank the very person she had so rudely spoken to earlier for helping her to calm down and making it possible for her to address her concerns with the principal. She even apologized for her angry outburst.

This event occurred during the time of the year when the Winter Olympics were being broadcast each night on television. After being thanked by the parent, the receptionist could not help noticing a T-shirt that the woman was wearing with a picture of an Olympic skater. They engaged in a pleasant conversation about the Olympics and the skater. The parent looked at the receptionist and asked, "Do you like this skater?" Without thinking, the receptionist replied, "I certainly do!" All of a sudden the grinning mother proceeded to pull off her shirt and toss it to the receptionist in full view of her children and several other people in the office. After saying, "Here, you can have it," the parent proceeded to walk out the door with only a sports bra covering her upper torso. The practical principal never knows what to expect from a happy parent.

The most remarkable aspect of this story was evidence through this illustration that every person in the school must feel included and comfortable in his involvement within it. The receptionist knew and understood her role in assisting even the most disagreeable parent. The other staff member, who instantly went and found the principal, knew his intervention was imperative in this instance. Upon her entry, the other parents and people in the outer office trusted in the abilities of the school personnel to address the issue. Ultimately, the principal understood that no matter how unreasonable the parent's harangue initially appeared, it was an opportunity to create and foster a positive relationship with a parent and build strong school ties for all potential future interactions. From a single negative event emerged an opportunity for an inclusive human, albeit humorous, moment to be shared by most of the participants affected by this event. In another school with another staff, the initial situation could have gone south in a heartbeat. The parent could have been arrested by law enforcement for disruption of school function or trespassing in full view of her children and others in the office. The end result of such an incident could have far-reaching negative consequences upon the children and their educational program, the witnesses to the event, and the parent herself.

Rather than reinforcing a hostile and negative relationship between the parent and the school, the principal and staff work together to create a positive alliance between all parties for the future. Every school has the potential to have disaffected, disconnected parents, students, and staff members working against the commonly held goals of the school. The transformational practical principal will seek to eliminate these negative possibilities and establish long-term lasting connections between all stakeholders to accomplish the best possible outcomes for every participant engaged in the process of educating our youth.

It is our hope and dream that this book in some positive way will assist its readers in becoming the type of leaders who will ensure that all students and staffs will realize their optimum potential together. We also hope that as leaders you will actively connect and engage students to participate in their public educations today, tomorrow, and throughout their futures. We wish you the best of luck in all your future endeavors as the practical principals of tomorrow. "You know you are a true leader when people want to follow you" (Gilliland 2005).

Bibliography

Gilliland, S. (2005). *Enjoy the ride: How to experience the true joy of life.* Charleston, SC: Advantage Media Group.

Schlechty, P.C. (1990). *Schools for the twenty-first century: Leadership imperatives for educational reform.* San Francisco: Jossey-Bass, Inc.

———. (1997). *Inventing better schools: An action plan for education reform.* San Francisco: Jossey-Bass, Inc.

———. (2003). *Working on the work: An action plan for teachers, principals, and superintendents.* San Francisco: Jossey-Bass, Inc.

———. (2005). *Creating great schools: Six critical systems at the heart of educational innovations.* San Francisco: Jossey-Bass, Inc.

About the Author

Deana Hollaway is a nationally certified and state licensed professional counselor with a doctoral degree in psychology. She has extensive experience in the public schools and enjoys working with young people and their families.

Werner Hollaway has been a recognized high-performing principal, assistant principal, teacher on special assignment, and guidance counselor within the same school system for twenty-nine years. He has led his schools with challenging student demographics and high poverty rates to improve their grades and aggregate student performance according to the State of Florida's School grading system achieving on multiple occasions the state's highest school grade. His most recent school achieved "adequate yearly progress" according to NCLB standards.